£2
⊃₂₂

Garry Disher was born
now lives in Melbourn
His many books includ
writers' handbooks, h
award-winning short stories have been published in
numerous Australian and overseas literary journals and
anthologies. He has been awarded grants and a
fellowship from the Literature Board, a residency in the
Board's Venice writer's studio, and the Stanford
University writing fellowship. *The Stencil Man* is his
second novel.

Other Angus&Robertson titles by Garry Disher include
*Flamingo Gate*, a novella and stories collection which
was shortlisted for the 1992 Steele Rudd Award, and *The
Bamboo Flute*, a novel for children, shortlisted for the
1992 NSW State Literary Awards.

IMPRINT

# THE STENCIL MAN

GARRY DISHER

Angus&Robertson
An imprint of HarperCollins*Publishers*

*AN ANGUS & ROBERTSON BOOK*
*An imprint of HarperCollinsPublishers*

*First published in Imprint in Australia by William Collins Pty Ltd in 1988*
*Reprinted in 1990, 1991 (twice), 1992*

*CollinsAngus&Robertson Publishers Pty Limited*
*A division of HarperCollinsPublishers (Australia) Pty Limited*
*25 Ryde Road, Pymble NSW 2073, Australia*

*HarperCollinsPublishers (New Zealand) Limited*
*31 View Road, Glenfield, Auckland 10, New Zealand*

*HarperCollinsPublishers Limited*
*77– 85 Fulham Palace Road, London W6 8JB, United Kingdom*

*National Library of Australia*
*Cataloguing-in-Publication data:*

*Disher, Garry, 1949 –   .*
  *The stencil man.*

  *ISBN 0 207 16958 6 (pbk)*

  *I. Title.*

*A823. 3*

*Cover illustration:* Desolation, internment camp, Orange, NSW
*by Ludwig Hirschfeld Mack*
*Typeset in 10/12pt Times Roman by Midland Typesetters, Victoria*
*Printed in Australia by Griffin Paperbacks, Adelaide*

*7  6  5*
*95  94  93  92*

This work was assisted by a writer's
fellowship from the Literary Arts
Board of the Australia Council, the
federal government's arts funding
and advisory body.

# PART ONE

# CHAPTER 1

When Martin Paul Linke saw the black Austin slow down by the pine trees at the cemetery corner and turn into his driveway, he knew what it was about. He continued to grub and turn the soil with his hoe: let them come to him. He heard the car's doors open and close, the chain rattle on the gate, and their boots on the hard paths between his rows of tomato seedlings. It was the fourth of September, the end of a winter of scanty rains. He straightened and turned around. He had lived in Australia for seventeen years.

The first man, a stranger, nodded. He wore his overcoat unbuttoned and held his hat in one hand. The second man said, 'Hello, Martin.' Today he had dressed in his captain's uniform and a greatcoat. Martin knew him as Frank Lucas, the mayor, owner of Lucas's Emporium in the main street. 'Martin, this is Detective Sergeant Bryant of the New South Wales Police Force.'

Martin Linke was certain that a third man had been in the car, but he could not see him anywhere, and, to his mind, that was the start of the dirty work.

'Frank, what's up?' he said.

'I'm very sorry, Martin. I've got no choice. We've got an internment order for you.'

Martin Linke put his hoe upon his shoulder, the sergeant watching expressionlessly, and said, 'I was expecting this, Frank. It is the fine British justice at work, locking me away in case I show Mr Hitler the way to Canberra.'

'We'll help you appeal, Martin. You'll be free in a year.'

Martin walked past him. The fellow's manner was false, he was enjoying himself in his VDC uniform. But put him back in his shop – in his shirtsleeves and braces, his bumpy skull catching the light as he grunted with a stick to fetch down a watering can hanging from a ceiling hook – and he was neither tall nor smart.

'You can have as much time as you like to wash and change and pack your things.'

'The great British justice,' said Martin.

The two men followed Martin Linke to the back door of his house. They waited while he took off his boots and washed his hands in the laundry trough. No one spoke. The third man was inside the house. Martin could hear him moving about.

There was a cardboard box open on the kitchen table. Martin looked into it, at his private papers, the interesting articles he had collected, his correspondence as president of the German Study Circle some years ago. He wondered how he was expected to appeal if they were going to take away all the evidence of his good character: his naturalization papers, divorce papers proving his wife's guilt, Christmas cards and letters from friends in positions high and low, even a card from Frank Lucas.

The detective sergeant left the kitchen and returned with the red, black and gold lacquered box in which Martin kept his sleeve links, studs and tie pins. Without speaking he took out a gold tie pin, held it up for Martin's inspection, and put it in an envelope in his pocket.

'We'll give you a receipt, Martin,' said Frank Lucas. 'Would you like to change your clothes now, and pack?'

This is the way it would be. Martin took his lacquered box back to his bedroom. How did they know about that particular tie pin? He had never worn it, after all. They had their information from his wife, well-known for her ways.

He took down a suitcase and folded into it a winter suit and other warm clothes, and, after some thought, lighter clothes for the approaching summer. He wrapped his slippers and shoes in newspaper and placed them, together with four books and his razor, strop, brush and lather stick, in a hollow between his suit and trousers. He took off his work clothes and dressed in his everyday suit, a clean white cotton shirt, a red and black tie, and shoes that kept a smart shine but were also sturdy. Who knew what indignities were ahead of him. An appeal hearing, a march through the streets, forced labour. He telephoned his brother-in-

3

law, for today had not been unexpected. He fetched his overcoat and hat from the hooks by the back door and said, 'Now we can go.'

As Martin Linke stood on his back step saying goodbye to his home, Paul and Nina walked around the side of the house, eager to see who was visiting. They stopped at once, afraid to come closer, swinging their school satchels. Martin put down his case, took their hands, and walked them away from the captain and the arresting officers, the so-called gentlemen. He blinked his wet eyes. Paul was desolate, he would not accept it, and Martin left him in the charge of his brave girl. He said, 'Your Aunt Jean and your Uncle Hartley will be here soon. Now, you must be good for them.'

He was thankful for the good people in the world who had not deserted him.

The two detectives sat in the front seat of the black car. Martin sat in the back seat with Frank Lucas. The drive to the police station took five minutes. Martin said, as they passed the flower beds outside the Institute, the shrubs and shaped lawns of the children's playground on the river bank, 'I did that. And that. Seventeen years, my God.'

At the police station Sergeant Richards said to the three escorts, 'None of this is necessary, you know.' Martin saw that he still had friends.

'You're responsible now,' said the detective sergeant, and he left, taking the other man with him.

Frank Lucas took off his captain's cap. 'Will you be all right now, Martin?'

Martin Linke – sitting in an office armchair and not on a cell bunk, drinking a cup of tea – said, 'Yes, thank you, Frank. I am among friends.'

'Don't be like that, Martin. I had no choice. You must have been expecting something like this sooner or later.'

'These are confusing times,' said Martin, leaning back in comfort. 'You had your orders to carry out. I understand.'

Mayor Lucas put on his cap and left, swearing.

'It's not right, Martin, it's just not right,' said Sergeant

4

Richards. 'But let us at least get your affairs in order.'

The train that was to take Martin to Sydney was due at seven o'clock. Sergeant Richards left a constable in charge and drove Martin to visit the bank manager, the pastor, two friends and his solicitor. They promised not to let the government take away his children or his house, or give the children into their mother's care.

At a quarter past six Sergeant Richards drove Martin home to say goodbye to the children. Martin knocked, but took his knuckles away from his door and said, 'Fancy that.' Jean opened the door and kissed his cheek. She was his wife's sister, proof that good and bad can come of the same stock. The children's clothes were packed. Nina was loading a box with toys and books, and Paul sulked about. The curtains and blinds were drawn. Then Hartley entered from somewhere, holding a broom, and asked Jean if anything else needed to be done. Is it no longer my house? Martin wondered. What more must I endure.

Sergeant Richards drove him to the station at ten minutes to seven. The dark night was very cold but there was no rain in it, only a wind that eddied the coal smoke when the express from Brisbane pulled into the station at seven o'clock.

# CHAPTER 2

Naturally everything had been worked out in advance – Martin imagined the telephone calls and the signals up and down the line – because Sergeant Richards took him straight up to carriage twelve and asked for Lieutenant McElroy. 'You'll sit there,' said Lieutenant McElroy, pointing at an empty seat. 'Keep the windows shut and talking to a minimum. If you want to go to the lavatory, ask first. Otherwise, no talking to the guards.' Martin saw him for what he was.

He pulled aside an edge of the window blind and watched the town recede. It was growing dark outside but no lights showed. Martin thought that the men in the carriage might be looking at him curiously, but they were all dozing miserably in the cold. They were Germans and Italians, but there was also one lone Japanese man with his own escort. Six other soldiers. And Lieutenant McElroy, the German-hater, a man who had no job of which he could feel proud. And no comfort for prisoners or gaolers. Martin turned up his coat collar.

The man sitting next to him said, 'I have some sausage here.' He was slight, an older fellow, opening a brown paper bag in his lap. 'Go ahead, take a piece.'

'Thank you,' said Martin. It was first-class sausage. 'This will restore a little of my strength.'

The man said that his name was Uwe Wurfel, from Cairns. 'Where the weather is beautiful most of the year.'

'Have you no warm clothes with you?' said Martin.

'I was stupid. I did not think.'

'Then you must wear the coat of my suit,' said Martin. He took his suitcase down from the luggage rack and opened it.

'What do you think you're doing? Are you deaf? Ask first.'

'I am fetching my suit coat for Mr Wurfel, who is feeling cold,' he said.

'Next time ask first.'

McElroy watched them for a while like a disagreeable dog.

'That is a terrible man,' said Uwe Wurfel later. Martin sensed that Wurfel was referring to things other than McElroy's manner.

The carriage lights were dimmed at nine o'clock. Martin attempted to sleep, but often he was awakened by his discomfort, and he saw each time that Wurfel was awake and thinking. Martin was troubled by dreams in which one misfortune was followed immediately by another.

He awoke at dawn and did not try to go to sleep again. He eased open the window blind, taking care not to disturb Wurfel, who was asleep against him, or McElroy, who probably could recite an edict about blinds. Life had slowed to a simple growl over the rails and Martin thought that he might stop and think now, but he forgot himself for the mists in the gullies, black and white cows getting to their feet, and here and there alarmed waterfowl. Then the train ran higher upon dammed earthen banks across swampy ground, and they were running alongside the Pacific Ocean. There were piers and small islands.

At seven o'clock the train stopped at Maitland for breakfast. All the men talked at once and the soldiers were sent to get sandwiches and tea. Martin asked, please, for wholemeal bread, and was told he'd be lucky. Lieutenant McElroy paced the length of the carriage and most of the prisoners stood up to arch their backs and roll their shoulders. They were unshaven, creased and puffy-faced; a sorry-looking crowd.

The tea was hot but too weak. The sandwiches were made from dry thin slices of bread smeared with bully beef. Uwe Wurfel twinkled in the face of this and brought out his sausage and his knife, and the two men plumped their sandwiches, their cold fingers craving and inept. 'Don't let them see the knife,' said Uwe Wurfel.

Martin had grown up in Bavaria, Wurfel in Saxony. Each man knew significant places in the other's district: a mountain, a lake, a village. 'My father died of wounds in 1916,' said Martin. 'I have not seen my mother since 1925. For three years now I have not been able to send her any money. What happens to the letters I post or the letters she posts? Who knows. What about you?'

'My father and my mother and I came here in 1905. I was sixteen,' said Wurfel. 'In 1915 they interned my father; now it is my turn.'

Lieutenant McElroy walked the aisle unhappily. 'He thinks we are plotting,' said Wurfel. 'Soon he will say no talking.'

The train stopped at Newcastle, where two Italian men were delivered to their carriage. 'They keep rounding us up,' said Wurfel. 'From everywhere. The innocent and the not so innocent. The loyal and the fanatical and those who don't know anything.'

Martin felt that he could ask, although it was not polite, 'And which are you?' but Wurfel only laughed.

'They have made their minds up, that is all that matters.'

'Will you appeal?' said Martin.

'I saw which way the tide was going,' said Wurfel. 'I will wait until it rolls back again.'

'I intend to appeal.'

'Good luck.'

The train crossed the Hawkesbury River and the men stopped talking. A tunnel closed on them like a clamp. They looked at one another in shock. The train passed into the light again, climbing through the mountains, rock-faces inches from Martin's eyes. Timbered folds and hilltops showed in the opposite window. They reached Hornsby station, a stage in the descent to Sydney, and then the hazy shapes became explicit. Most of them had never seen the harbour or the famous bridge. Martin said:

'One could forget that one was a prisoner under guard.'

'An internee under guard,' said Wurfel.

At the central station they were ordered to leave the carriage and form into lines on the platform. Men in the adjacent carriages were also prodded into lines and counted. Like sheep, Martin thought. The soldiers here had bayonets fixed to their rifles. An ugly weapon, and not at all necessary. Civilians – free civilians – stood watching. 'Put this on,' a soldier said, giving each man a grubby thin coat marked PW. Some of the spectators cried out; they shook their fists, one old man shaking his fist at Martin alone. Martin stepped up to the tongue-lashing man. 'You don't understand,' he said. 'We are not war prisoners.' He wanted everyone to know that. The man gathered himself to strike Martin and a soldier said, 'Step back.' He had a rifle, it had that bayonet stuck to the end of it, keeping civilian separate from civilian.

The internees were taken away from the tumult, out to the street, where buses waited to take them to the Liverpool camp.

Wurfel whispered in Martin's ear, 'Don't give them cause. Never give them cause.'

# CHAPTER 3

Sixty-three men stood in their underclothes on the cement floor of a long iron shed. Some of the men smelt unwashed. Vests and underpants drooped or were holed or grimy. From observation and conversation Martin learned that most of the men were Germans and Italians, but there were also two Lithuanians, a Finn, a Dane, and two Australians of British descent. He wondered what they had done wrong. As Uwe Wurfel had said, they came from all over the country, trainloads of new internees every week.

They stood in two rows, holding their bags or cases in one hand and the clothes they had been wearing in the other. One by one they shuffled to a bench halfway down the shed, where soldiers turned them around by jabbing their shoulders, eyed them up and down, squeezed and separated their clothes and personal things. They found Uwe Wurfel's knife; Martin heard him say mildly, 'It will scarcely cut through the skin of a sausage,' but it did him no good. A searcher flipped the pages of Martin's books and turned in inquiry to an officer, who shrugged. Martin thought that they were all ignorant and would rather be playing two-up. It was also very cold in the shed but the soldiers did nothing to speed the search.

A nurse led Martin into a tarpaulin cubicle. Here were people who cared. The doctor asked him to cough, he was X-rayed and inoculated, and they sat him down to talk about his diet. A nurse wrapped him in a blanket. Martin sat hunched, giving himself an area of blanket on which to rest his nerveless feet.

He got dressed and passed on to the quartermaster's bench at the end of the shed. 'Overcoat?' said the quartermaster. 'Boots? Socks? Shirts? Trousers? Underclothes?'

'I would like another coat,' said Martin.

'Another coat, he says. No can do. You can have what you need, not what you want, and every man gets two towels, blankets and sheets.'

Martin could only shake his head. He gathered a bundle of bedding and went outside, where he found Uwe Wurfel waiting for him, overwhelmed in the folds of a new black overcoat. 'Here is your suit coat,' said Uwe. Martin put the suit coat on under his overcoat. He thought that his feet would never be warm again. 'We have not eaten since seven o'clock,' he said loudly.

An officer said, 'We'll show you to your huts first and then you'll be taken to the mess hall. Try and be patient.'

'Thank you,' said Martin. He exchanged smiles with Uwe.

The discipline was less strict here inside the camp. While they waited for the last of the sixty-three men to leave the shed, other internees came up to greet friends or ask for news. Men shook hands and shouted and the Italians had tears in their eyes. Martin had to turn away and look up at the sky and breathe deeply: he was far from home now. And, quickly, his misery intensified, for, beyond the wire, women and children were looking at them from a separate compound.

He said to a young corporal, 'Those children and women. Are they interned also? Who are they?'

'Just women and kiddies,' said the corporal. 'Some of them've got husbands in here.'

'Are there children there by themselves, without a mother?'

'That I wouldn't know,' said the corporal.

'Do you think the authorities could intern my children?'

'Don't ask me,' said the corporal.

'They were born in Australia, their mother is Australian, and I myself have been naturalized.'

'Tomorrow morning why don't you go along to the administration block and talk to them there? They'll tell you. Any morning.'

'I will go this afternoon, after we have eaten.'

'No you won't,' said the corporal, throwing down his cigarette butt. 'Mornings only. Look, I'll be around the place tomorrow

11

morning after roll call, that's at half past nine, and I'll take you there myself.'

Martin held out his hand. The corporal, surprised, leaned out of his habitual slouch and shook hands with him. 'Thank you,' said Martin.

The next morning Martin looked for the corporal. He didn't know how he could exist another minute in this place. Last evening he had had to rinse his plate and cutlery in a copper boiler of heaving scum. The cook was a grubby careless man. Men played cards or smoked or talked after dinner and two fights broke out, probably over politics. The camp was too crowded, and no two men shared the same beliefs, but of course the authorities could not see that. There were National Socialists trying to influence the German nationals and the young Australian-born Germans. Martin was reminded of the men who, when invited to speak about modern Germany to the members of the Study Circle, had been intemperate rather than informative. Established internees resented the newcomers. Even the warm-hearted Italian men whom Martin had met on the train and in the inspection shed were touchy and would not talk to him. All this he had learned in one evening. And where was there evidence of a committee or any sort of leadership?

'Sir,' called Martin. The corporal was smoking a cigarette and watching two internees coating a stone border with white paint.

'Over here,' said the corporal. Martin followed him to the administration huts. 'Stand in the queue,' said the corporal. 'They'll fix you up in there.'

'Thank you,' said Martin, but the corporal had left. If they are not German-haters they are graceless, he thought.

A terrible place. The men in the queue caught Martin's eye and turned away as though to spit. They seemed to be saying: He's been here one day and he thinks he can come along and tell them a story and they'll set him free. Uwe Wurfel was all Martin had, but Uwe had been put in a different hut, and Uwe was a man who watched and waited.

The line moved forward and then it was Martin's turn. Major

Orr was fumy and addled from a cold in the head. He asked Martin his name, held his hand to his back while he found Martin's file in a wooden cabinet, and sat down to read.

'How can I help you?' he said after a while.

'There are two matters, my children and my appeal.'

'If you appeal now, the earliest we can hear it will be halfway through November,' said the major.

'I must wait until November?'

'Everyone is appealing, Mr Linke. The court of appeal is small and overworked.'

'Two months,' said Martin.

'Shall we submit an application?'

'What happens if my appeal fails?'

'It is possible you will be sent down to a camp in Victoria,' said Major Orr.

'You can do that with people's lives? Move them from place to place like sheep and cows?'

'Mr Linke, we're at war, and you are classed a borderline risk.'

Martin said, pointing to himself, 'I'm not at war. I'm not at war.'

'We are thinking of your own safety as well, Mr Linke.'

'My safety?'

'There have been incidents,' said Major Orr, passing a form across the desk. 'Fill this in when you leave here and bring it back to my office tomorrow morning. Now, what's this about your children?'

Martin thought, keep a level head.

'Yesterday I saw the women and children through the wire and my heart fell to a very low state. I want to know, can you do that to women and children, and what will happen to my children?'

Major Orr blew his nose and massaged his temples. Every effort wasted him away and he should have been in bed. He said:

'Didn't you make arrangements for them in case something like this happened? Surely you did.'

'All this,' said Martin, 'and now you say I am also a bad father.'

13

'That's enough, Mr Linke. Where are the children now?'

'With my wife's sister and her husband.'

'Is your wife with them too?'

'My wife is an immoral waster whom I divorced before much damage could be done. The children must have nothing to do with her, but what can I do from in here? It is well known that innocent children can be poisoned against their fathers.'

'I can't help you with this matter,' said Major Orr. 'If their aunt and uncle are good people I'm sure the children will be all right.'

There were more ins and outs to the problem but the major was not prepared to listen to them.

In the afternoon Martin obtained a ruled ledger-book, which was better than nothing, and in the first half he wrote about his life and his contribution to his town and community. He has been called 'a borderline risk': very well, they will have evidence and they will see which side of the border he stands. He turned the book upside down; working from the back page, he constructed a case in defence of his right to his children.

# CHAPTER 4

The internees were allowed visitors on Thursday afternoons. The lucky ones were men with families in the women's and children's camp or living close by. Of course, no one came down to see the Queensland men, and nor did Martin expect anyone to come down from his district, but one Tuesday Major Orr sent for him. 'Your sister-in-law is here to see you,' he said. 'I'll make an exception this time, but please tell your family Thursdays in future.'

A guard took Martin to the special hut. Jean sat at a table on the other side of a barrier: wire netting in a wooden frame, Martin noticed. They tried to kiss through it, and Jean held his hooked fingers before she sat down. She took off her mittens.

'You haven't brought the children with you,' said Martin.

'Travelling's impossible, Martin, you've no idea. I was lucky to come myself.'

'I mustn't complain,' said Martin. 'I'm very grateful. Are the children well?'

'Extra well. They did these for you.' She rolled a letter and a crayon drawing into cylinders and poked them through the wire. Martin looked around at the soldier standing guard.

'The major's seen them, it's all right.'

'I'll save them for when you go,' said Martin. 'Do my letters arrive?'

'Sometimes two in one day, sometimes none for two weeks. They must keep them for a while before they pass them.'

What would make her come all this way? Martin looked at her hands and at the walls and Jean smiled and said, 'Well, here we are then.'

'The vegetables will need regular watering,' said Martin. 'We get the newspapers in here. I know how dry it is everywhere.'

'Hartley looks in every day. Martin, someone's broken windows and painted things on the walls.'

He put his palms down on the table top. 'It's ridiculous, isn't it. That is the psychology outside the barbed wire. Here inside the barbed wire there is another psychology – '

'But not to worry,' said Jean. 'At the cannery there's a widow with three children desperate for somewhere to live, so we've arranged for them to rent your house. A nice woman.'

'A widow? What happened to her husband?'

'Oh Martin, I didn't like to ask. Now, Hartley arranged with Mr Campbell to withdraw some money from your account to pay for new windows. I hope that was all right?'

'Yes, yes,' said Martin. 'But I don't know what you will do when everything is ripe. How will you know when to pick? This is what happens, do you see that?'

The wire thickened, smelling of iron. Dusty coils and imperfections. A plaster woman sat wearing a brown dress, grey coat and flowered scarf. Martin Linke saw her plaster hand move, creeping over a woollen mitten. The wire receded to a lace of cobwebs again. It was Jean, after all, something constant in his life.

'Do you have something to tell me?' he asked.

'You're not to dwell on it, but Betty did pop in last week to say hello. It's all right, the children were at school. We had a heart to heart and I told her she can't expect to come along after all this time and see them.'

Martin shouted, 'I thought so!'

Jean's hand leaped to her heart.

'Now she will say that I am unfit,' cried Martin, 'but she is the unfit one. She can't have them. You tell her that.'

'It's no good shouting at me.'

'That was the judgement of the court. Your sister's ways are well known. Those buggers took away my papers but I have written about it, the total case against her.'

'I can't act as if she doesn't exist,' said Jean. 'But I was firm with her. I said we were the children's guardians now until this all blows over.'

16

'Two years ago she said it was the shame of the investigations, but she's not too ashamed to come back when I am powerless and think she can give the children another father.'

Jean leaned towards the wire. 'Keep your voice down, for heaven's sake.'

Martin laughed spitefully. 'Walls have ears.'

The guard said, 'Your time's up now.'

# CHAPTER 5

It was a Sunday afternoon in spring and the internees wrote letters or read or slept on their bunks. The days were warmer but an unsettling wind blew outside, like the Föhn in Bavaria which cleared the haze obscuring the Alps but brought with it a malaise that made the people tired and cross. Martin Linke had thought of Bavaria more than once lately.

The letters he was re-reading lay scattered around him on the bed. He was thinking about barbed wire disease, wondering if his inability to disentangle the issues in his life were a symptom of it. Barbed wire disease took the internees in various ways, but mostly you knew the victims by their air of inaction. Perhaps, like him, they were simply waiting for a blur to clear.

He picked up another letter, from Nina, and read:

*'I am in the same bedroom as Margaret and Paul is in the boy's bedroom. It is a bit crowded but all right. Paul is all right now except he tries to get out of school but he is not really sick. I am well and I hope you are too. Thank you for the letters which Auntie Jean reads out because of your writing which is hard to read sometimes. Thank you for doing the stencil drawings, they are nice. I put the castle one on my composition book except I don't tell the kids it's Germany.*

*'A lady from the cannery Mrs Wood is going to live in our house plus she's got three children too. Some boys assaulted the house, I know who but it will be all right now Dad. Auntie Jean makes us feel at home also Uncle Hartley. The description of the camp was interesting and your friend Mr Wurfel but I will be glad when you come home again. Dad it's not really a prison is it? which Margaret says it is but I tell her no. I must close now.'*

Martin gathered the letters, put them back in an old shoebox, securing the lid with string, and returned the box to the shelf next to his bunk. A crayon drawing from Paul hung tacked to the wall above the shelf. There were children's drawings on walls in every hut in the camp. In addition to houses and trees the children drew fighter planes tangled in combat, smoke and flames, faces, swastikas back-to-front, bayonets sticking in. It was Uwe Wurfel's view that children everywhere had been seized by an infection. Martin, alarmed, had started sending his son and daughter stencils of shapes and scenes popular when he was a child in Bavaria.

Martin sighed. He did not feel like writing a letter today. He was allowed two letter-cards per week, twenty-two lines in each, read and tampered with by the authorities.

Finally he reached for his ledger-book and fountain pen, compelled by the notion that his notes would bring order to the disorder in his life. There wasn't a day in which he didn't feel this idea nagging him. He might be occupied with a stencil or conversation or simply staring into an empty coffee cup and have to go to his ledger and open it.

He turned the pages. He did not write. He had nothing but repetitions to add to the character defence in the front of the ledger and his right to his children in the back of the ledger. And somehow the woman who had been his wife was mixed up in both matters. That confused him. There were things he wanted to say about his farm, his clients, the drought, his house, the people living in it, and his children's future, but he did not know whether to write in the front or the back of the ledger or in both places. He wanted to kick out the walls and knock his enemies down.

# CHAPTER 6

On the twenty-second of November Martin was summoned to Major Orr's office and told that his appeal would be heard on the twenty-seventh. He sent his lawyer a telegram. Mr Wainwright had promised to represent him at the tribunal free of charge.

At eight o'clock on the morning of the twenty-seventh a bus took Major Orr, three guards, and Martin and eight other men to the city courtrooms.

They stepped out of the bus. The Liverpool air was sour; here the air seemed unused and benign, and the internees smiled in a cluster on the footpath while the people ambled by. Car windows and chromium reflected the sun. The women and girls wore summer dresses and some of the men carried their suit coats over one arm. Martin took off his suit coat. The newspaper vendor on the next corner apparently preferred yarning with a streetsweeper and a sailor to calling out the war news. Martin watched people drop their pennies into his outstretched palm and help themselves. He thought that if he were asked now to assess the country's morale, he would say *inattentive*. He did this from time to time, imagined a report to a spymaster. He used not to do it.

The men were taken into the building. Their heels clacked along the waxed corridors and Martin was conscious of his trousers scuffing. He held his case notes against his chest.

In an anteroom to the appeals court the men waited their turn. A Finn was first, twenty minutes later a second Finn was called in, and then a Lithuanian. Major Orr accompanied each man into the court to give a brief report. Clearly they were hearing the six German men last. Here is competition, thought Martin. He looked at his notes. All his categories seemed wrong, all the facts were in fragments that would have him turning pages like a madman.

'Sir,' he said, when Major Orr had come back from the courtroom, 'I must meet first with my lawyer. Will you please take me to him. I think that is just.'

'Wait here,' said Major Orr. He left the room and walked down the corridor.

'I must meet first with my lawyer,' an internee said in German.

'The matter is very grave,' said another.

'Please, sir, will you take me to my lawyer,' said a third.

Martin retorted sharply.

A guard stepped away from the door. 'Come on, you fellows, what's the joke.'

Major Orr returned. 'Mr Linke, will you step into the corridor for a moment, please?' He said gently, 'I'm sorry, Mr Linke. Your lawyer doesn't seem to have arrived yet.'

Martin made an immense gesture. 'Five days ago I sent him a telegram.'

'Perhaps he's been delayed. In any case, I'm sure you'll be given a fair hearing.'

The men in the anteroom knew that something was wrong. They looked at the floor. They could be unkind but only to a certain point. Martin sat down. He felt obscurely ashamed and could not think clearly.

Martin Linke's appeal was the last to be heard. A judge and two associates sat at one table in the courtroom and three uniformed men and a civilian sat at another. A stenographer gravely waited. Major Orr explained to Martin the name and role of each person. One officer was the prosecutor, the other two were from military intelligence. The civilian, Mr Feinstein, from Germany, was the interpreter. Martin sat straight in his chair and said that an interpreter would not be necessary and he felt like saying that there would be no justice if that particular fellow were a judge and not an interpreter.

The prosecutor said, 'Major Orr, perhaps you'd kindly give the court your statement now.'

Martin looked away from the prosecutor and towards Major Orr. Then he looked at the judges' bench. He was uncertain of the proprieties. He didn't know where he should be looking or to whom he should eventually address his remarks. He looked at Major Orr again.

'Martin Linke arrived at the Liverpool Internment Camp on the fifth of September 1942,' said Major Orr. 'His conduct in the weeks since then has been exemplary. He spends his days reading and writing and walking the perimeter with a friend, Uwe Wurfel, who, incidentally, was sent to Tatura recently. To the best of my knowledge Mr Linke belongs to no faction and has no connection with any of the camp's troublemakers. His only letters have been to his children and their guardians, his sister-in-law and her husband, and they expressed the normal concerns of a father and a man who has had to leave behind a business. Many internees try to see me time and again, usually for spurious reasons, but, apart from casual meetings in the grounds of the camp, I have had only one meeting with Mr Linke. He came to see me on the sixth of September to express concern about the welfare of his children and make inquiries about an appeal. He received one visitor, his sister-in-law, on the nineteenth of October.

'In conclusion, I should assess Martin Linke to be a gentle fellow, a man unlikely to pose any real security threat.'

'Thank you, Major,' the prosecutor said.

Major Orr smiled at Martin and left the room. He seemed to leave traces of his troubled, scrupulous spirit behind him. Martin released the table edge, and sighed, and looked from face to face.

The prosecutor began:

'Mr Linke, you arrived in Australia in 1925, settling first in Western Australia?'

'Yes,' said Martin. 'Life was very difficult in Germany after the war.'

'And you spent how long in Western Australia?'

'Almost one year.'

'What work did you do?'

'Fellows like me were sent to clear land for farms. I worked alongside many young men from Britain.'

'In 1926 you moved to northern New South Wales. Why?'

Martin said, 'I wanted to go to an established district where the land was cleared, towns, roads, good water supply.'

'You wanted a head start. Did you resent the opportunities being offered the British migrants in Western Australia, Mr Linke?'

'No, of course not. There is room for everybody.'

'You've lived near Casino since 1926?'

'Yes.'

'How would you describe yourself. Your profession, I mean.'

'I own a small farm, part of which is orchard, part is for vegetables and seeds common in Europe but not so common here. There is a demand for these items in Brisbane and Sydney, you know. I have many business contacts there.'

'Would you call yourself an ardent Nazi, Mr Linke, or merely sympathetic?'

Martin was confounded. He believed from the question that he could only be one or the other. He pushed his ledger a short distance across the table and said something indefinite.

The prosecutor said, 'You take a keen interest in the shire, I believe?'

Martin recovered and said, 'I was a councillor for five years. I made the memorial garden and the park. I give the young people jobs. When the school and the church are raising funds I give.' He folded his arms. 'Those are the things you should have in your reports.'

'When were you naturalized?'

'In 1928.'

'Why have you appealed against the internment order, Mr Linke?'

'Because it is unjust. In 1940 Inspector Burton of the police and your Captain Marks from the military intelligence questioned me and examined my affairs and they were satisfied I am a loyal citizen. Since then many kind citizens send the police to my door when I have visitors, saying there is a house full of foreigners meeting, but I am still a loyal citizen two years later. My God.'

'Where did you get the tie pin, Mr Linke?'

23

'The tie pin?'

'The tie pin bearing the German flag. Where did you get it?'

'Am I back in the Middle Ages?' said Martin. 'Is this the Inquisition?'

There was a movement on the judges' bench. 'That will do, Mr Linke. You will kindly answer Captain Walker's question.'

'A business acquaintance in Sydney sent it to me. I did not ask for it. I have never worn it and I have never wanted to wear it. You got your information from my wife. My God, if that is typical of your sources.'

'I think Captain Atwood can shed some more light on this matter,' said the prosecutor. 'Captain Atwood?'

The officer from military intelligence said rapidly, 'The tie pins were imported from Germany by one Maximilian Joseph Brinkerhoff, formerly of Neutral Bay in Sydney. Brinkerhoff's interests included a restaurant, a hotel and an import-export agency. From 1936 he was involved in printing a German-language newspaper and inviting members of the Nazi Party in Germany to address Germans living here in Australia. He sailed for Germany in July, 1939.'

The prosecutor said, 'Did you know Brinkerhoff, Mr Linke?'

'Only as a fellow businessman. He bought things from me for his restaurant. I put them on the train and sent them down to Sydney. The other things I know nothing about.'

'But he often gave you things like the tie pin and you subscribed to his newspaper.'

Martin appealed to the judges, 'The war had not started then.'

'Nevertheless,' said the prosecutor, 'you took a keen interest in Hitler's Germany.'

'I only subscribed to the newspaper to be polite,' said Martin. 'I admit I was a little interested because my mother and uncles are still in Germany, and I had memories of how bad it was there after the Great War, but I was never like Brinkerhoff and the others, no.'

'Yet between 1936 and 1938 you operated a German Study Circle in your district. Captain Atwood?'

24

'The German Study Circle met every two or three months in the homes of Martin Paul Linke, Klaus Heinrich or an Australian sympathizer, Michael Kevin Burke. The average attendance was twelve, although attendances began to decline in 1938.

'Topics discussed at these meetings included "The Miracle of Modern Germany", "The Ayran Contribution", "Adolf Hitler, his Philosophy and Achievements", and various less specific topics such as German art, music and literature.

'On the second of October 1936, Dieter von Neher, of the German consulate in Sydney and also a member of the National Socialist Party in Germany, spoke to the members of the German Study Circle on "Germany's Resurgence, the Role of Germans Abroad". On the tenth of May 1937, Nicholas Stuber, another member of the Nazi Party, this time a visitor from Germany, read a paper entitled, "The Jewish Conspiracy". There are other examples, your honour.'

Martin Linke proffered his wrists. 'Yes, yes, it's all there and more,' he said. 'Take me and put me against a wall to be shot. Who was the fly on the wall, I wonder?'

'Mr Linke,' said the judge. 'Please limit your remarks to the matter at hand.'

'Would you like a glass of water, Mr Linke?'

Martin nodded abjectly. Everyone watched the prosecutor fill a tumbler with water from a glass jug. Martin moistened his lips and tongue.

'You must have a thorough knowledge of your district, Mr Linke.'

'Yes.'

'Do you own a camera?'

'Oh sure, since 1936 I have been sending Herr Hitler snaps of my children's school, the public lavatories, the weeping willows on the river and Sergeant Richards burning the weeds in his garden.'

'I take it you do not consider yourself a threat to security?'

'I have been saying that since 1940. I don't want to say anymore. Today I have seen more of your great British justice at work. Yes, I will bow down before it.'

'You don't want to tell us anything about the pamphlets? Captain Atwood.'

This Captain Atwood was like a nasty bird pecking. 'In December 1941 we received a report from number three Base Post Office that they had recently handled about five hundred copies of a pamphlet entitled "Where Do I Find My Church", addressed to Army personnel by name. Other post offices reported a similar traffic. The pamphlet bore no printer's imprest, but carried a complete list of Lutheran churches in Australia and pastors with their telephone numbers.'

'Well, Mr Linke?' said the prosecutor.

'Well what?' said Martin. 'Now you are saying God is a security risk, is that it?'

The second intelligence officer leaned forward and said, 'The pamphlet was withdrawn from circulation on the grounds, Mr Linke, that any unsuspecting soldier might ring the phone number of a pastor, thus revealing his unit's location, which would then be passed on to a central organization.'

'Thank you, Lieutenant,' said the prosecutor. 'I'm sure we don't need to bother Mr Linke with the particulars of our work.'

The officer blushed. 'Oh. Yes. I see. I beg your pardon.'

'Well, Mr Linke?'

Martin said, 'I was helping my church, that's all. The pastor asked me. I don't feel very well.'

The judge said, 'Yes, Captain Walker, I think we need not detain Mr Linke in this court any longer. Sergeant, would you take Mr Linke outside please?'

'I have notes here,' said Martin, trying to rally. 'You have not heard yet my appeal.'

'It is precisely because you appealed that this hearing was convened, Mr Linke,' said the judge. 'Our task has been to hear the grounds upon which the Commonwealth challenges your appeal, and invite your responses to these. Thank you, Sergeant.'

Martin was led to a small room. The guard shut the door and leaned against it smoking a cigarette. Martin sat down. After a while he began to look at his hands as an archaeologist might look at muddied implements. They were useful hands but not clever, and he was the only one who could see that. Someone knocked on the door and he was led back into the courtroom.

The judge said immediately: 'Martin Paul Linke, it is our judgement that the Commonwealth's order of internment against you, issued under the attorney-general's hand on the third of September, 1942, is sustained. You will remain in internment until, in the opinion of the attorney-general, your being at liberty will not prejudice public safety or the defence of the Commonwealth. I imagine that in a year or so you may apply for a reassessment. In the meantime, notwithstanding your naturalization, long period of residence and contribution to your community, we find that, owing to your past associations and activities, over a number of years, there is a small but unacceptable degree of risk in your being at liberty. However, I might point out at this juncture that it is apparent you were misguided in some actions and unaware of the implications of others. Clearly you were, or are, a small cog in the machinery of German fifth column activity in Australia. It is even probable that your interest in Hitler's Germany was at first quite innocent. Nevertheless, the internment order stands. I would remind you that you are not a prisoner. You are an internee, entitled to all the privileges that that entails. Sergeant, would you . . .'

Martin was taken to a different waiting room. Some, but not all, of the other internees were there. He looked at his watch: they had dealt with his life in just twenty minutes. At half past twelve Martin and five other internees were taken by bus back to the camp.

Later that day Martin happened to see the three missing internees standing at the iron gates, carrying suitcases and shaking hands with friends. He wondered what their stories were.

# CHAPTER 7

Gangs of construction workers came into the camp every morning. By the middle of December the compound was cramped with new huts. As fast as one man was sent to Hay or Tatura, two would arrive to take his place. Sometimes a Japanese family – a husband and wife, children, an elderly relative, a European spouse – passed through the camp, escorted at bayonet point. The food got worse and the canteen often ran out of little comforts and necessities. The internees grumbled and sometimes struck one another. There was little else for them to do. One quiet man leapt screaming onto an officer's back for no apparent reason.

On the nineteenth of December Major Orr called Martin into his office. 'Time to pack your things, Martin,' he said. 'You're going down to Tatura.'

The next evening Martin and a number of German and Italian internees and two Japanese families were driven to the Liverpool station, counted, and put aboard the Sydney to Melbourne express. No German-haters this time. The internees shared their food and talked to the guards, and Martin even saw a woman escort officer jiggle a Japanese baby on her knee. They were permitted to open the windows.

By dawn the train was near the border. At Albury the internees were counted and put on another train. The new train ran into Victoria and down through the wheat plains. Every paddock had a hopeless horse in one corner and the hollow sheep panted from stubble patch to stubble patch, raising dust, or stood hesitant before the cracks on the dams. Once there was a cow sunk to its udder in mud, a woman in overalls tugging its horns. She released the head, plunged around to the hindquarters, twisted the tail, but the cow heaved uselessly, and the woman rested herself across its back and could have wept. In one or two places men sealed

28

a few bags of wheat with needle and string. No one looked up. Martin thought that it was worse than the newspaper pictures suggested. There were things he must write to Hartley about right away.

At Seymour the internees were taken off the train and handed to the Victorian military authorities. Again they were counted, but then left to themselves. The train pulled out of the station. In the station yard three military transport trucks and a van waited under gum trees, the drivers playing cards in the dirt, their hats pushed back. A farmer tumbled a sack onto the tray of his buckboard and drove away. People rode past on bicycles. It was going to be a hot day; Martin could smell the peppercorn trees. He felt hungry and aimless. The internees had not eaten for fifteen hours.

An army jeep drove fast into the station yard and stopped behind the ticket office. While the driver kept the motor running, an army officer helped an elderly Japanese man get out of the jeep with his luggage. The officer led him to the Japanese family groups, where he was greeted with polite bows and nods by the young men and women. The officer returned to the jeep and the driver sped them away. 'All right, time to go,' said the officer in charge of the guard.

The Japanese boarded the first truck, the Italians the second and the Germans the third. Their seats were wooden planks. The van carried their suitcases. The little convoy left the station yard and pushed north-west for fifty miles, grinding and juddering through dust that took everyone's breath away. It was impossible for them to talk, or play cards, or read, and the country was not worth looking at. 'Punishment indeed!' shouted Martin, but no one ever looked at Martin when he spoke elliptically.

The convoy slowed down a few miles from the town of Tatura and the truck carrying the Japanese internees turned right, onto a track leading to a cluster of half-completed buildings inside a high perimeter fence. The luggage van followed it. The truck carrying the Italians continued down the road. Martin's truck turned left and crawled alongside an irrigation channel for several miles before turning off the track and stopping outside a set of heavy gates.

'This is it,' said a guard. 'The German camp.'

The men stepped down from the back of the truck. Guards and officers saluted one another, papers were handed over, the internees were counted again. It was all familiar to them. Of course every soldier had a bayonet on his rifle. Martin wanted to stamp his boots in the dirt and shout 'Boo!' unexpectedly at one of these warriors, to see what he would do.

The luggage van lurched in and two soldiers unloaded the luggage, placing it in three rows along the ground. The officer receiving the internees said, 'I am Lieutenant Dinham. You will kindly go to your luggage and open it for inspection.'

Martin said, 'Yes, there was a German spy behind every haystack throwing us bombs and guns.'

At once, every internee took it up: 'See,' they said, 'my buttons are a secret weapon. There is invisible ink in my pen. My tobacco tin is a radio transmitter.'

A small group of internees watching from inside the camp began to whistle and jeer. Dinham and his soldiers stood alert, waiting, Dinham with his hand on his revolver butt. The internees behind the wire saw this and cried, 'Buffalo Bill!'

The noise stopped, Martin and the others stepped back from their bags, and the soldiers began the search. Martin's mirth subsided but he had not felt so good for days.

'That's better,' said Lieutenant Dinham. 'Now, when I call out your name and the number of your hut, you may enter the compound. As you can see, there is a welcoming party waiting to show you around. After lunch in the mess hall you will meet your camp-leader, Dr Oser, one of our first internees.'

Dinham read through the list. When it came to Martin's turn to walk into the compound, he sensed Dinham's hard stare. He was reminded of Uwe Wurfel's advice, 'Never give them cause,' but told himself he did not mind. If he made the most of each day, a year would soon pass. A voice said, 'Hello, Martin.' Confronting him was a small, balding man, Uwe Wurfel looking ill and much older despite his sunburnt face. 'I see that you have been noticed already,' Wurfel said.

# PART TWO

# CHAPTER 8

Martin was made so alarmed by his mood on Christmas Day that he started to keep a daily journal, using the middle pages of the ledger-book and telling himself not to look at the other sections. He called it: *My Life at Tatura.*

He began:

At 6.30 the bugle sounds for us to get up, wash and shave ourselves, and get dressed. Bugles and time bells rule our lives, we are like puppets. But I fight a little fight against them because I rise at *6* o'clock. I wave to the sleepy men in the watchtowers, 'No, Mr Guard, I am not escaping. Do you think I want 21 days in the bunker?' I walk across to the latrine, and then to the shower block, quite alone, greeting the best part of the day, before it gets too hot. There are many birds about, crying out and rising and settling near the irrigation canals and the reeds and lakes. Rosellas, white cockatoos, mallee parakeets, wrens, ducks, cormorants, all kinds. When the sun goes down at the end of the day, back they come again. I walk past the flower beds on the parade ground, pat one of the stray cats, chase the rabbits out of the vegetable gardens. One last look at the distant blue mountains.

I am at the shower block. I can shower in peace at this hour. There is nothing like a cold shower to wake you up, or cool you down later in the day. I scrub myself, keeping my toes away from the scum in the corners of the cement floor. Someone has not mopped up properly. I shave, and comb my hair. I have some grey hairs, which in a normal life would not appear so soon. Time to get dressed now, so back to my hut in my trousers and braces, put on a clean shirt, take off my slippers and put on my shoes.

7.30, that damn bugle again. Men call out to each other and we all stream like cattle across the compound, up the 'street' to the mess halls for breakfast. Eggs again, but there is a choice of jams on the table by the serving hatch and someone has picked flowers for the tables. I have noticed this, that men away from their homes will create a substitute home. Men stitch cushion covers and we all want pictures for our walls. I have sold many stencils that way.

So I have a bedroom, a bathroom and a room to eat and talk in, like any man in a house, only there are no doors from room to room in my house, the rooms in my house are hundreds of feet apart.

The men at breakfast. There are those who are alert and ready to face the day and those who are bad-tempered and morose. But there is no sleeping in for anyone. Just look out if you miss breakfast because at 8 o'clock the guards come in to count us. 'Where is Mr Linke?' they will say. 'Not in the hospital, not released, not escaped, not on kitchen duty, not at breakfast? Then it is the bunker for 24 hours when we find him,' they will say.

The next bugle is at 9 o'clock. Those on duty stay behind to wash the dishes, some of the lazy ones go for their shower and shave now, some don't bother, but by 9 o'clock everyone is standing at attention by his neatly-made bunk, everything shipshape, ready for roll call. Who is it today? Sergeant Loman. 'Hut 14, all present and correct, sir!' Never far away there is a rifle with a bayonet on the end of it and it would not do to misread that casual pose.

9.30. Three hours until it is time for lunch. How does a man while away the hours. That depends on temperament. I have observed human psychology here and first there is the man who needs some outside order or guidance. Maybe he is a no-hoper. Maybe also the days are too long and he knows he will go mad if he stops to think.

For such men there are work projects outside the camp, they are marched out under escort to work on civic projects, roads, bridges, timber cutting. For a joke they are called Empire Builders, building things for the British Empire. Under the Geneva Convention we are not compelled to work, but it is available for those who want it. Six hours a day, for two shillings a day, that is fourpence an hour. Atrocious pay. I myself do not need this outside order in my life, and also I will not sell my labour power for fourpence an hour now after earning 2/9 an hour for contract work at home.

I asked Uwe Wurfel why he joined the Empire Builders. He ignored the question. I have thought about it. Strangely, he can feel alone out there sawing wood with a hundred other men.

The next type is the man who prefers to call his time his own. These men form the largest group. You see them reading, washing their clothes, writing letters, talking, sleeping, studying, eating pastries and drinking coffee in Cafe Wellblech (Corrugated Iron). They are not all no-hopers. This is the trouble, people make hasty judgements. If a man is pushed and pulled by bugles and time bells every hour of his life, if he is locked up away from his loved ones and familiar surroundings, he doesn't want to give himself over totally. Nevertheless, the discontented are here too, 'prison lawyers' who distract you with advice, men who steal your boots for the leather, men whose intentions I am sorry to say are unnatural, men who endlessly confide, and always one or two men marked for death from illness or by their own hands.

To do nothing is not suited to my temperament and so we come to the third type. Professional men, craftsmen, gardeners, men with a trade. There are garden plots for those that want them, and workshops where one can construct toys, furniture and brass items. Three men make bowls and vases and fire them in the kiln behind the kitchen. Two men are pastrycooks. Another is a barber, another mends shoes, two men run the library. There is the camp newspaper, *Brennessel* ('Stinging Nettle'). We have five professors, two from Sydney University, one from Adelaide and two among the German nationals sent here to relieve the pressure in the English camps. These men give lectures in the schoolhut, they are the top men in their field. I have had many interesting talks with Professor Steiner, a professor of linguistics in London when the war started.

My time is occupied with gardening and making stencils, both earn me a few copper and brass coins of the camp currency. Strangely now I prefer stencil making. I begin with the design marked on cardboard or if I am lucky a thin sheet of metal, then I cut or punch out the design, and when the stencil plate is ready I place it on the paper and wash ink, paint or a water colour over it. The satisfaction is supreme. I have designed a windmill with curved blades like sails, a wolf looking back at you, a horse and jinker in the snow, a church steeple, a stretch of the Bavarian Alps, a giant and a gnome, a man with a certain hat, and a castle with turrets. No doubt Nina and Paul think them strange, such shapes are unknown here. What a difference there is between what I see in my memory and what I see in the light of the sun.

If a man is rostered on duty the day is quite a different matter. In rotation, three huts are on duty for two days. First thing in the morning we clean the gutters, latrines, washhouses, shower blocks and laundries, and pick up paper and other rubbish. It is like living in a village, no not really. After the 9 o'clock roll call it is off to the kitchen to wash and peel the vegetables, chop up the meat if we are having stew, and make large pots of tea and coffee to pour out at lunchtime. Then cleaning up and washing the dishes. After that we have three hours free, then back to the kitchen, help prepare and serve the evening meal, clean up afterwards. The same the second day. There are men who hate duty roster. They grumble and do as little as possible. I just laugh. They cannot understand that in a community as large as this we must work together and have regulations or we would be at each other's throats quick smart.

If we feel unwell the morning is the time for sick parade at the hospital hut, or maybe we will have to fall in for an address by the commandant. He is not respected.

12.30. Lunch bugle. This is a sight to see, mobs of men rushing to the mess halls. No matter how busy or fulfilled we are, we live for the next meal. Breakfast, lunch and dinner are the highlights of our day. It is understandable, deep down we are unhappy, eating makes us feel better, it takes us out of ourselves. Why else do I see some poor fellows spending all their spare tokens on pastries from the pastry hut?

1 o'clock. The Empire Builders have one hour's rest now, we others may sleep, read, or spend the afternoon working. More often than not because of the unrest there will be a hut search now that we are sluggish from eating. The afternoon is also the time to let off steam or take your grievance to Dr Oser if it is an internal matter, or the camp commandant in the administration hut in the military garrison if it is more important. Usually I read a little, then do some work, it is a good balance that way. From my observations if you have rest, keep active, avoid thinking of the sex impulse, and have an optimistic frame of mind you will last. If not you will fall by the wayside.

3.30. Time for the post. Another charge of the light brigade, this time to the post-office hut. Our names are called out in alphabetical order. How can we whose names are far down the list stand the suspense? I don't know. Will there be a letter from Nina, Jean, Hartley? Will there be good or bad news about the farm and my affairs? Are the children happy and well looked after? Is the guidance there to steer them away from unhealthy influences? These are the questions I ask myself as I wait for a letter to be delivered into my hands.

I check the date always. When was it posted? Before you got my last letter, naturally. That is the chief problem, the delays and misunderstandings, the lost opportunities, the explanations required. What did you mean by this, my dear Nina? What did you mean by that, Mr Campbell? Yes, getting letters is a torment and a joy. I understand why some men dig tunnels or climb the wire.

The 5 o'clock bugle sounds. The Empire Builders are escorted back to camp, the rest of us drift back to our huts to shower and change, or maybe first we meet for a game of tennis, handball or skittles, or perform exercises under the guidance of an instructor.

Now it is 6 o'clock and I am writing these confidences. Later I will read a newspaper from home and watch the birds return to the waterways when the sun begins to settle. I will find some fellows born in Bavaria and we will talk about Munich, the opera, our schooldays, the sorts of things we ate. I can't stand the way it is always war news war news war news or politics at the centre of every conversation. I might try to talk to Uwe Wurfel, but it will not be easy, he has made enemies, he doesn't listen, you have the uncomfortable feeling that he knows you inside and out whether you are a friend or not.

7 o'clock bugle. Respects to the dead, then roll call, then dinner. We

eat well, I must admit. To my mind it is because we have first class chefs who have worked in the top restaurants of Europe and Australia. They can make anything tasty. Perhaps it will fall off later with war shortages, they say it will.

What to do until the final bugle at 9.30. We are never at a loss here, unlike the situation in Liverpool. Depending on the day of the week we have a concert, a play, a film, a slide lecture or a meeting in the entertainment hall. Sometimes we have music and songs from the camp orchestra. There are two evenings when nothing formal happens, Thursday and Sunday. There are many interesting conversations going on however because amongst us are doctors, professors, sailors, rich and poor men, educated and uneducated, European-born, Australian-born, some Finns and Danes, radicals and conservatives, and last but not least National Socialists. Of course there is not a man among us who believes he should be here. Last week I talked to a missionary from New Guinea, the week before that to an Olympic skiing champion. Tonight it might be Theodor Egk, Oser's deputy, interned by the British in Kenya, and a man best avoided, I think.

9.30. The final bugle. Across to the latrines one last time, with the searchlights poking in the dark corners nearby. What happens to the human waste? I know what happens to some of it, some of it finds its way to our gardens.

10 o'clock. In bed, lights out, or it's the bunker for you, my boy. Eighteen men, including snorers. It is the luck of the draw. What I have drawn is a mixed lot, full of strife and differences and dominated by a rowdy element. Today I went to the leader of Hut 26 to request a transfer to his hut because I have friends there, men from Bavaria. 'Where were you born?' 'Bavaria.' 'Are you a German subject?' 'No, I am now a British subject.' 'This hut is reserved for German subjects.' I happen to know that there is no such regulation here. It is an example of an unwritten law, of course such things go on and you can't do anything about them. I could only shake my head to realize I don't belong inside the camp or outside it.

# CHAPTER 9

On New Year's Eve Martin received a letter forwarded from the Liverpool camp. It was from Mr Wainwright, his lawyer, explaining that his request for legal representation had not arrived until the day after the tribunal. Mr Wainwright promised to help Martin with any future appeals and said he knew Martin would be pleased to know the farm's affairs were all in order. 'I'll see you in a year,' he wrote.

It had been Martin's resolution to start anew in Tatura, but the letter did its damage. In the course of the afternoon he convinced himself of dirty work by the authorities, that Wainwright was crooked, that Betty had the children, that the postal service was slipping and the country with it. The day seemed to have no end to it.

Martin crossed the compound to the pastrycook hut and bought two German pastries with the currency he'd earned from the sale of his tobacco allowance. He then took the pastries to the mess, ordered a cup of tea, and sat down alone. Many of the internees were sharing items from their food parcels or smiling over their letters and it was unendurable. Out of the clear sky had come the old feelings. He finished and went outside.

Half past three in the afternoon in the middle of summer. A dull punch of heat from the corrugated-iron huts forced him away from the buildings, towards the trees. He heard the wooden huts tick in the sun; bark and twigs peeled and snapped in the gum trees.

He walked through the deranging air to the barbed wire entanglement inside the perimeter fence and looked out at the Great Dividing Range and the Victorian Alps, dim like paint smudges above the paddocks. The names unhinged him. He lifted his fist. 'Little Dividing Hill. Australian Alp. Victorian Alp. Shit to you.' He turned on the irrigation lakes and channels. 'Piddle, puddle,' he cried.

The guard in the closest watchtower leaned out. 'Get away from there. Get out of the heat, you mug.'

Martin hooted and waddled rapidly up and down the edge of the barbed wire entanglement, trailing his knuckles in the dirt. 'Just a poor ape in a cage,' he said. 'Just a poor ape with barbed wire disease.'

After a while Martin agreed to bugger off. He found Uwe Wurfel sitting alone in the mess.

'You look pleased with yourself,' said Wurfel.

'I almost lost my nerve this afternoon,' said Martin, 'but I feel restored now.'

From behind a wall of discouragement Wurfel said, 'I'm glad to hear it.'

'Are you all right?'

'Don't worry your head about it, Martin.'

Internees drifted into the mess during the afternoon, avoiding their hot iron dormitories; more men, tormented by mosquitoes, came in at nightfall. But it was also New Year's Eve. The cooks had been secretive all day. Men in the brass band whistled whenever their paths crossed in the compound and a notice on the noticeboard promised surprises in the evening.

At six o'clock the bugle signalled the start of an hour's drill and inspection of the guards in the compound. The internees' restlessness and the clip and tramp of two hundred soldiers' boots worked on Wurfel's nerves. He muttered. Martin wanted to counsel his friend; it was as though their roles had been reversed.

Finally Wurfel stood up. 'Excuse me for just one minute, please,' he said, and walked among the tables to the gramophone in the corner. He selected a record, fitted a new needle from the tin, wound up the machine, and set it going, weighing all his movements. Beethoven's Fifth Symphony scraped unsteadily into the room. Wurfel returned to their table. 'That's better,' he said.

A few minutes before seven o'clock Dr Oser and his bully boys entered the mess and sat at their usual table, looking keenly at everyone. Someone stopped the gramophone. Uwe Wurfel, enraged, remained seated when the bugler played the Last Post. Dr Oser and his henchmen noticed, as they noticed everything that went on, and they looked at Martin, too, making connections.

After roll call Dr Oser stood upon a chair and raised both his arms. 'Men, men,' he said, smiling and looking around at the internees. The camp-leader was never without a thin black walking stick, tie and ironed white shirt, or the company of Theodor Egk, his aide, a man with a bony, unhappy face. Camp rumour said that Egk once knew Hitler, had run with his brownshirts. Martin was prepared to believe it: Egk said little but his enforcers and agents were always about, putting fear into the doubters and taking aside the susceptible. Martin had felt Egk's assessing eye upon him since his little show of defiance at the camp gates the day he arrived, but now Egk had seen him in the company of Uwe Wurfel, who was more than a doubter. Dr Oser spoke on, Egk at his side looking long and hard around the room. 'May our fortunes change in 1943,' Dr Oser said. He asked them to remember the blood that flowed within them, the land of their fathers, the Fuehrer. Before Martin was quite ready, many internees had clacked together their heels and extended an arm in salute.

It was time to eat. Martin remarked to Professor Steiner, who stood next to him in the queue, that the German people knew how to enjoy themselves. The cooks brought in bowls of sausages, dumplings, spiced pork and beef, horseradish, cheese, butter, salads and bread rolls. On the walls there were flags and pictures suggestive of a beer hall, for one of the surprises was barrelled beer, enough to give each man a pint, three enamel cups full, which he sipped and let roll over his tongue to make it last. It was easy to imagine that one was growing merry. The men ate and drank and shouted for songs from the opera singer, an Austrian trapped in England at the start of the war. The brass band played folk songs and drinking songs. In the quiet moments between bursts of singing Martin talked to the professor about matters of culture and society.

And then later the professor made an excuse to leave him and Martin became aware of two men standing behind his chair and he heard Egk say confidingly, 'May I sit with you for a moment, Herr Linke?'

Egk sat down in the professor's chair. The other man remained standing.

'Dr Oser himself asked me to speak to you,' said Egk.

'To me? About what?'

'Please, it's nothing to get alarmed about, Herr Linke. We try to meet every new internee in person, and there are some, like you, whom we think deserve some words of appreciation for the work they have done.'

'Me?' said Martin Linke.

'We know of your contribution. We also know how easy it is to lose hope in here, to be swayed by what others might say.'

Egk stood up. He leaned over to shake Martin's hand and said, 'We must talk again soon, Herr Linke. May I wish you a happy year in 1943.'

'And you,' said Martin automatically.

At twelve o'clock the internees sang in the new year and walked back to their huts, singing up at the guards in the searchlight towers. The men in Martin's hut stayed behind to sweep the floors and wash the dishes. It took them an hour. On his way back to his hut afterwards Martin stopped at C latrine block, where he knew he could urinate in peace, and it was there that he found Uwe Wurfel bruised and bloodied on the stinking floor. 'Oser's secret police,' said Wurfel. 'Who do you think, Martin?' He did not want to be taken to the hospital hut. Martin washed away the blood and, like drunken clowns pinned down by spotlights in a circus tent, the two men stumbled across the compound to Uwe Wurfel's hut.

# CHAPTER 10

One day the editor of *Brennessel* approached Martin and asked him to make a stencil for the paper. Apparently a sailor in the hospital hut suffering with a recurring condition had written his own account of the battle at sea between HMAS *Sydney* and the German raider *Kormoran* in November 1940. 'We'd like to illustrate the story,' said the editor.

Martin had no idea what a large warship looked like. He wanted to be accurate. He went to the hospital with a pencil and several plain paper sheets.

Sailor Greiff had been singed by flames; half his head was hairless and unnatural; but Martin's visit stimulated him and he sat up, smiled, and began to weave atmosphere into the threads of his story. Martin pulled his chair closer.

First he sketched *Sydney* making the challenge. It is four o'clock in the afternoon, in the Indian Ocean 120 miles off the coast of Western Australia. The *Kormoran*, wearing camouflage, is flying the Dutch ensign.

'Not the Norwegian ensign,' said Greiff. 'The Australian newspapers were incorrect.'

The watch reports that a warship has appeared on the northern horizon, steaming towards them at full speed. Within half an hour HMAS *Sydney* has closed the distance and she stands to, 1000 yards off, signalling.

'Not quite face on,' said Greiff. 'We could see a little of her flank.' He took the pencil from Martin's hand. 'The *Sydney*'s guns were like so, and the *Kormoran*'s funnels should slope a little more.'

At once the *Kormoran* brings down the Dutch flag and hoists the German ensign and fires a salvo, and another, every shell finding its mark on the *Sydney*. Greiff can see outbreaks of flames and smoke. The *Sydney* is sluggish in the water, firing single shots which fall short until the gunners have the *Kormoran*'s range. Perhaps only five find their mark on the *Kormoran* before the *Sydney* retires, burning from stem to stern.

'There was damage to her bridge and wireless station, here and here,' Greiff said. Martin pencilled alterations to the *Sydney*'s superstructure.

But the *Kormoran* is critically hurt. The oil tanks are holed, the oil drains away, there is no power, no response to commands from the bridge. The captain gives the order to abandon ship. It is six o'clock; visibility is still good.

Martin drew the *Kormoran* stopped on the surface of the sea, splintered holes and fire damage in every lifeboat.

'So we inflated the rubber boats,' said Greiff. 'Some had seventy men in them. No provisions. One boat capsized and sixty-eight men lost their lives. Those of us still on board watched them drift away towards the coast.'

It grows dark. Greiff and the other skilled men who remain on board the *Kormoran* set time charges in her hold, winch a wooden skiff out of the hold and into the water, and finally abandon ship. At midnight they see the flash of the explosions, then hear them, and feel a swell move across the sea. Behind them the entire northern horizon glows red as cloud banks and the ocean reflect the *Sydney*'s fires.

'We sailed for eight days,' Greiff said. 'I didn't know at first that I was burnt or had an injured leg. The sun and salt were cruel on my poor skin. In some of us the doctor made incisions, in others he put stitches.'

A small coastal steamer sights them.

'Don't talk to me about man's humanity,' Greiff said. 'They did not take us on board, they towed us with a cable, at speed. The sea washed in and we slid on the planks in agony, afraid that we would be swept overboard. Ten hours, this lasted for. They trained guns on us. Did they think we would rise up out of our watery condition and climb along the cable and overpower them? When we made port we could not even stand. You should be drawing this too, Herr Linke.'

But Martin had begun to see the picture he wanted. The backlighting is the *Sydney* in flames far away. In the foreground there are men outlined in a lifeboat, hunched watching the *Kormoran*, her stern high out of the water at the moment of her slide into the depths.

Martin said goodbye to Greiff and left the hospital, stealing some pain-killing powders on his way out. He took them for Uwe Wurfel, who continued to get headaches from his beating two months ago. It was bright in the sunlight. The lunch bugle sounded.

At the end of the quiet hour between one o'clock and two o'clock there was a disturbance, a distant, unsettled noise: '*Haussuchung. Haussuchung.*' Soon men in every hut took up the cry. It was the signal to hide radio transmitters, receivers, knives, alcohol. It gave energy to men in a torpor after their lunch. Martin laughed. Here and there, he was sure, dirt was whisked away with a twig broom and the lid placed over a tunnel. Hut search. Martin put his sketches in the box under his bunk and went outside to watch.

Lieutenant Dinham and a troop of soldiers came fast through the gates, the soldiers streaming to left and to right until they had ringed Hut 5. The occupants were brought out and told to disperse. National Socialists lived in Hut 5, friends of Theodor Egk and Dr Oser. 'Buffalo Bill, Buffalo Bill,' said the internees.

At Martin's elbow Uwe Wurfel said, 'There is rumour of a tunnel under Hut 5.' He was smiling as he watched.

Martin understood at once. 'It is a mystery where these rumours come from,' he said.

'Who can you trust?' asked Wurfel, opening his arms.

'Please be careful,' said Martin. 'By the way, I have here a preparation to soothe your headache.'

The two o'clock bugle sounded; it was time to go back to work. Uwe Wurfel put the powders in his pocket and said goodbye. The men of Hut 5 had gathered nearby, angrily indicating their blockaded hut to Theodor Egk. Soldiers had been seen carrying in crowbars, levers and hammers. The authorities could be very thorough.

Martin went back to his drawings. Later in the afternoon he made a stencil and delivered it to the editor. 'Perfect,' the man said. Martin helped him set the page and operate the printing press and by seven o'clock they had their newspaper.

During dinner conversation Greiff's story vied for attention with the news of the outcome of the search on Hut 5 – a tunnel that was only a few feet short of the wire. The next day the authorities announced a three months' ban on outside war news and other privileges. They seized copies of *Brennessel* and dismantled the printing press. When Greiff's injuries stopped weeping they took him to the Prisoner-of-War camp a few miles away. He said he was merely a sailor. They said he had been employed under war service. From time to time they brought him back to the hospital, always placing a guard on his bed. Dr Oser protested that the banning of privileges was collective punishment and therefore illegal under the Geneva Convention. Privileges were restored. Unnamed assailants left Uwe Wurfel bleeding in the darkness once again.

# CHAPTER 11

The long summer ended at last and autumn began. Martin Linke worked in his garden and sometimes he made a stencil for one of the other internees. He rarely saw Uwe Wurfel, who now avoided everyone. Martin wrote his two letters each week and occasionally he received one. He liked to read his mail while drinking tea in Cafe Wellblech, and it was here that Theodor Egk said, one day in April:

'I have been remiss in not having had that talk with you, Herr Linke. May I sit down? Forgive me – please finish your letter.'

Martin put the letter in his shirt pocket. 'It's all right, I was reading it for the second time.'

The letter contained discouraging news. Apparently Betty had turned up with a cake on Paul's birthday, and the authorities were requesting changes to the farming of Martin's land. 'It's to help the war effort,' Jean wrote, 'or so Frank Lucas informs us.' Things were falling asunder behind Martin's back.

He attempted to concentrate. Egk was saying how important letters were as a link with the outside. Somehow even he had managed to get a couple of letters, written by his wife and delivered with the help of the international Red Cross. 'But letters cannot provide everything we need.'

Martin's attention was caught by the fellow's expressive hands, which had expressed the order to destroy Uwe Wurfel's nose and spirit.

'The New Year's Eve party was a success, wouldn't you say, Herr Linke? Apart from the food and happy mood it gave us a chance to be Germans publicly. Would you like another tea or coffee, Herr Linke?'

Egk had the skill of steering encounters. Martin said, 'Thank you, tea please,' before he could think about it.

Egk walked away among the tables in Cafe Wellblech and came back with biscuits and two cups of tea.

'A terrible pity about the newspaper,' he said.

'Yes.'

'Your picture was very vivid. Many men commented favourably on it.'

'Unfortunately there was little we could do about the smudging,' said Martin. 'We were not set up to make a proper block from the stencil.'

'Still, it was a gesture. It helped in its way to bring the camp together. No, I'm serious, Martin – may I call you Martin, Herr Linke? – there are divisions in this camp when we should be acting as one. I'm sure you know what I'm talking about.'

Martin looked around the hut but no one seemed interested in why Egk was sitting with him, and Uwe rarely left his bunk these days, leading a dim, sad, unheroic sort of life.

'Will you appeal against your continued detention here, Martin?'

Martin said firmly: 'Yes.'

'Naturally you will,' said Egk. 'I can understand that. You have lived in Australia for many years now, Martin. Your roots are here, just as mine are in Germany. But, don't forget, your government has seen fit to treat you as an enemy alien and put you in a concentration camp.'

Egk's words focussed Martin's trouble and pain. 'The great British justice,' he said sourly.

'Exactly,' said Egk.

'They think they can take away my children and land.'

'What they can't take away from you is that you are a German,' said Egk, holding tight to Martin's arm.

After a while Egk said, 'You can help me in little ways.'

'I know what you're doing,' said Martin. 'But I must keep my hands clean or they will reject my appeal again.'

'Just in small ways, Martin. Nothing that will draw attention to you. For example, next week we celebrate the Fuehrer's birthday, April the twentieth. Some suitable designs to put on the walls would be nice. After that we have the elections for camp-leader, hut-leaders and the management committee. It would help us if we knew what the men were thinking.'

'A spy,' said Martin. 'Is that it? You want me to spy for you?'

'Spy? No, I don't think so. Look at it this way: there is no cohesion, German subjects sit with British subjects, Lithuanians with Danes, Jehovah's Witnesses with other crackpots. The authorities think to themselves, divide and rule, and we say unity. A firm hand is needed.'

'Dr Oser's hand, no doubt.'

Egk's face grew close and private. 'We will be putting his name forward again,' he said.

'They destroyed me in court at my first appeal,' said Martin. 'They made the smallest incident sound like a big treason.'

He looked convulsively at the internees drinking tea and coffee in Cafe Wellblech and said, 'We have been seen talking like this and it will go in my file and come out at the tribunal how I was a Nazi strongman. No, no.'

He took with him the empty cups and saucers and left them in a clatter on the table by the serving hatch. Outside Cafe Wellblech the internees had not ceased to idle or toil or the drowsy guards to flick cigarette butts out of the watchtowers, but clearly the spies and informers were not about to declare themselves. Bowed by the pressure of their eyes upon him, Martin hurried to his garden and picked weeds all afternoon.

In the days that followed he spent his time cautiously sleeping, eating and working. He turned the garden soil and wished for good rains this year, here and in the north. He sat alone in the mess. He tried to make stencils of gum trees for his son, but abandoned them in favour of legends and the power of his mind's eye. There is nothing distinctive in the gum tree shape. He did not make stencils for the National Socialists and they did not contact him again. No letters came for him. The tone of his diary was deliberative.

But all that week men were at work transforming the small sports ground and the entertainment hut. On the evening of the

47

twentieth of April, drawn by the hubbub and seeing no profit in his abstemious state, Martin emerged to celebrate the Fuehrer's birthday.

They remembered the dead. Dr Oser and the men of his committee, holding flaming torches above their heads, led the internees along the dark avenues between the huts and then across the compound to the sports ground. The torchbearers stood on the rim of a semi-circle painted in white in the dirt, the internees arranged themselves in rows behind them, and everyone looked towards the flag rising on a white flagstaff. A bugle sounded. Martin wept a little, his feelings engaged by darkness and stillness and the press of his neighbours' elbows.

The mood held. The men stood rigid, entranced, on the sports ground in the dark until, at an order snapped by Theodor Egk, the torchbearers filed off the painted ring. The men sighed. In speechless disorder they broke ranks and walked back across the compound to the entertainment hall.

Trestle tables, rocking from the weight of treats from the kitchen, lined the walls. Electric lights illuminated paper streamers, flags and portraits of the Fuehrer. In the place of the stage backdrop was an immense swastika, its unsparing black arms clenched in a red field. The internees stood and looked at it.

'Are you seduced, Martin? Does your heart swell to see this?'

'Oh,' said Martin foolishly. 'How are you? You must be feeling better.'

'You could say that,' said Uwe Wurfel.

The damage to his nose had affected his speech. He looked smaller; Martin could see the knocks and scrapes on his pale skull. A troublesome nerve briefly pulled his head about. From his appearance and voice Uwe Wurfel might have been one of the feebleminded.

Wurfel returned Martin's stare and then he said, 'Do you feel contempt for me, Martin, in all your good health and ecstasy?'

Martin threw his arms about. 'I'm just pleased to see you up and about,' he cried, until Uwe restrained him, saying, 'It's all right, Martin. Let us get some food and find a quiet corner.'

They sat and talked, Martin laughing sportively and often, consumed still by his friend's question. Some time later, Dr Oser walked up to them and stood looking at their faces and plates of food, his hands resting upon the silver handle of his black stick. Theodor Egk and two other men waited nearby, dressed alike in gleaming boots, sharply pressed grey trousers and shirt, and berets fashioned from red blankets. Dr Oser knocked the point of his stick against the floor once or twice. Martin had no idea what Egk was thinking.

'Birthday parties are a fine thing, Dr Oser,' said Uwe. 'Don't you agree? Handsome uniforms,' he said to Theodor Egk.

Dr Oser walked away. A moment later Egk followed him, first telling the men in the red berets, 'Stay and watch these two.'

Dr Oser climbed the steps to the stage and raised his stick above his head. 'Today is a special day,' he said when the internees had stopped talking. He told them why. Martin Linke and Uwe Wurfel sat listening in their corner of the hall, flanked by the men in the red berets. There was singing until ten o'clock, and one or two rallying cries. At the end of the evening, when everyone was leaving the hall, Uwe tugged the sleeve of a man who had stood watch over them and said, 'Did you think I would spoil your party? Foolish fellow!'

A week later Martin and Uwe returned to the entertainment hall to witness Dr Oser's re-election. The Party had also been successful in the voting for hut leaders and camp management committee. In his address to the internees afterwards, Dr Oser said that he felt very encouraged by the unanimous showing of hands for each man nominated by the Party. In the days that followed the election a number of new notices appeared on the noticeboard. One notice explained that owing to the increasing complexity of internal matters some sort of policing was necessary and so a special force of men had been appointed. The internees would know the officers by the red berets they would wear while on duty. On the next film night Martin, Uwe and four other men were stopped at the door by men wearing the berets and told that their cinema rights had been suspended for the time being. Uwe

Wurfel was thrown out of his hut and when it was clear that no other hut would take him in he moved a bunk into a room in the schoolhut. He tried to cut the wire once but the guards caught him and locked him up in the bunker for twenty-one days and if you saw his face afterwards you would say the likelihood of his rallying again was remote.

# CHAPTER 12

On the first of May they celebrated Europe's greening with market stalls, German food, entertainment and singing. In the morning a number of wooden benches, which had been constructed in the workshop, were carried down the hill and set up around a maypole, the sportsground flagpole which had been extended with a length of bamboo and festooned with paper streamers. Martin decorated his stall with hessian dyed yellow and green, and he displayed a range of his stencils, and snapdragons, leeks and pumpkins from his garden. The man next to him sold ashtrays and letter-openers fashioned from brass shell-casings. Another man sold bookends and carved animals. One man had painted watercolour pictures of the camp, and he also offered to draw your portrait while you waited. There were hourly performances by acrobats and clowns who had been with Wirth's Circus before their internment. The pastrycooks sold out of cakes and buns and had to close their stall while they made a fresh batch. The fortune-teller wore a black cape and a cone-shaped hat with silver stars painted on it. Between telling fortunes he sold tickets for the lucky-dip, a bin of donated goods and items from Red Cross parcels, each wrapped in coloured paper. The men in the red berets had approved each stall, but there were two complications later, once when Professor Steiner was knocked down for distributing international-labour leaflets, and once when Lieutenant Dinham, on an off-duty stroll with the camp commandant, became disagreeable at the brass-smith's stall and impounded his letter-openers.

At midday the stalls were closed and the internees boarded lorries and set out for a picnic. The picnic site, chosen by Dr Oser and the commandant, lay on the other side of Tatura, but the lorry-loads of internees, food hampers and brass band instruments stopped first on the outskirts of the town. The internees clambered off the lorries, formed into ranks behind the brass band, and began to march down the main street. The day was to be more than a simple fair and picnic: it was the view of Dr Oser and the camp commandant that the huge camps were a part of the district's way of life now, and should not be denied. The brass band trumpeted, the internees stepped high and true, while in the passenger seat of the food lorry Uwe Wurfel watched spiritlessly, and Lieutenant Dinham kept pace with the marchers, his hand near his holster.

It was Saturday, almost lunchtime, and the street was crowded. Townspeople and women from the outlying orchards and wheat farms shopped with their coupons or stood talking under the shop verandahs while their children played tag between the cars and buckboards. Bored airmen from the base and off-duty guards from the prisoner-of-war camps wandered in pairs or stood smoking outside the hotel. Once or twice a girl walked by and they took their cigarettes away from their mouths.

People stared, some muttered, when the brass band and marching internees drew closer. A reversing farm truck braked, shaking loose a pat of mud from its axle. Small boys imitated the trumpets.

An airman threw the first tomato. He snatched it from the crate at the greengrocer's door, pushed aside an elderly man holding a child by the hand, and leaped into the street; but his throw was weak, as though he had grown embarrassed at the last second. He yelled indistinctly. The tomato broke open on the road, splashing pips and juice over Martin's shoes, and the internees marching near him cried out and got out of step.

'Murderers!' shouted a woman. Children searched in the gutters for stones. To Martin, every face was vengeful, every eye had alighted upon him.

The soldiers and airmen faded back among the ill-natured shoppers, and reappeared with apples, tomatoes and potatoes. One airman, his arms full of apples, cried exultantly to the grocer, 'We'll pay you after,' and plunged after his friends.

They ran onto the street, closed in on the internees, and threw vegetables and fruit in nipping attacks, sometimes in a kind of savage dance with their victims as they manoeuvred for a clear shot at heads and testicles. Martin was knocked towards the footpath, where hands spun him around and pushed him away. The children threw their stones, and a child punched a beer bottle against a man's leg. Martin protected his face with his arms and ran, doubled-over, back to the lorries.

'Stay here!' shouted Egk, attempting to hold him.

Egk, no longer still and assessing, flourished his red beret. He lunged with his men into the crowd, hitting out at servicemen and women carrying parcels.

Lieutenant Dinham blew his whistle. 'Everyone onto the trucks.' The guards spread out and advanced. 'You've had your fun, boys,' they said.

Martin turned away from the struggles and thrusting faces and, without knowing why, stepped onto the running-board of the food lorry. He hung there panting, looking in at Uwe Wurfel. 'I got hit,' he said. Wurfel nodded, or it might have been the tic in his face. The corporal raced the engine a little. 'You can't hang on there,' he said.

The battle had been ragged and brief. As the convoy drew away from the town, the internees pressed against the rails on the lorry trays, saluting risibly, the salute that was conquering Europe in the newsreels. One man beat his drum and bellowed and the trumpeters blew their trumpets. Behind them, children picked up the scattered fruit, and on the footpaths the airmen and soldiers, all elbows, said 'Excuse me' to women loaded with shopping bags. The internees felt the wind in their faces. They grinned.

The lorries arrived at the picnic site and the men jumped to the ground. By now they were very hungry. They wandered among the trees looking for firewood, or helped the cooks spread ground-sheets and set up a trestle table. The guards leaned against the lorry cabins, rolling cigarettes and clowning with the internees about the fight. Some men spoke to one another for the first time.

No one moved far away from the fire. It was not because they were being overly obedient, or respectful of the commandant's trust in them, or mindful of Buffalo Bill's ugly hue and cry at their heels. With luck and cunning they might have crossed paddocks and stepped through broken fences and reached Melbourne, or swum the irrigation channels and hitchhiked to Sydney. But they could not shake off the habit of the barbed wire entanglement and the perimeter fence.

Lunch was called. Like the inhabitants of crowded islands in a grassy sea they clustered on the tarpaulin groundsheets with their sandwiches and tea. The soldiers stood guard without troubling to hold their rifles. From a stool next to the fire, Uwe Wurfel wordlessly kept the water boiling and the tea fresh. He had not been asked to do it. He would leap up to pour the tea, and then sit again like a carven figure.

Martin lingered with his second cup of tea, gradually losing the sensation of encircling barriers. He stretched his legs and leaned on his elbow; he could easily sleep. There were shadows, almost too cool to lie in, but sunlight always followed as unheard winds in the stratosphere pushed cloud masses across the sky. He thought about the fight in Tatura. It bore no relation to letters or newspapers from home and he wondered what was being hidden from him.

'Shall we go fishing, Martin?' said Professor Steiner.

Martin returned his empty cup to the table by the fire and began walking down to the river with Professor Steiner. Uwe Wurfel stared into the coals.

They passed Lieutenant Dinham buttoning himself at a tree. 'Fishing?' he asked.

'Yes,' said Professor Steiner.

'Don't wander off.'

Six red-faced men lumbered past them, unused to the grass and uneven ground. They carried stones and branches. At the river bank they emitted cries and converged on a rabbit and beat it to death.

'Last winter,' said Professor Steiner, pointing into the distance, 'those mountains had snow on them. I expect it will be the same this year. I was reminded of Germany most strongly.'

'So you have been here almost a year?'

'Almost a year.'

His fishing rod was a length of dowelling from the workshop, with a catgut line and a crusty hook. The two men dug for worms in the damp soil. Martin was surprised when they found some. Professor Steiner put the worms into a small tobacco tin, saving one for his hook. Because his line was so short he sat as close as possible to the water. Martin squatted to keep his haunches dry. The river water was motionless except for insect ripples here and there.

'Did you do this when you were a child?'

'Oh yes,' said Professor Steiner. 'I was the Huckleberry Finn of my town.'

Martin could not imagine it. The professor sat heavy and sacklike on the river bank, his only vanity the fastidiously shaped beard.

'Dr Oser chose well,' the professor said.

When Martin did not reply he said, 'This picnic site.'

'Yes, it's very peaceful.'

'He has an eye for beauty.'

Martin said clearly, 'Yes and no.'

The professor laughed. 'It's all right, Martin. I'm not attempting to trap you.'

'The elections were farcical,' said Martin. 'And they've taken away my cinema privileges.'

'They won't let me enter the library,' said Professor Steiner. 'No doubt we've been noticed talking together today.'

'They banished Uwe Wurfel. They won't allow him to move freely in the camp.'

'Herr Wurfel,' said Professor Steiner, 'is nothing but an embarrassment.' He raised his fishing rod until he could see the worm on the hook. 'Still there. I don't believe there are any fish in this river.' He sighed. 'What an uninspiring country this is.'

Farther down the river another internee and two guards were

also fishing. Other men slept in the grass or walked, head down, with the professor of botany. On the slope behind Martin and Professor Steiner a large group of internees played American baseball with a tennis ball.

'Martin, would you like to come to a meeting tomorrow night?' said Professor Steiner.

'A meeting? I didn't see the notice.'

'You misunderstand me. Four or five of us are meeting to discuss what we should do about Oser and Egk.'

'I don't know,' said Martin.

'I thought you might be interested. But consider it and tell me if you would like to attend. Of course no one must know about it. Perhaps I have said too much.'

'I feel no love for that crowd,' said Martin.

'Many do.'

Professor Steiner raised the hook out of the water again. 'Gone. I didn't feel anything.' He rebaited the hook and dropped the line into the water. 'I have been talking too much and forgetting to twitch the hook.'

Martin stood up. 'Good luck. I should see if Uwe is all right.'

'Tell me if you decide anything,' said the professor.

Martin skirted the baseball game. There appeared to be Egk's men on both teams. Either everyone was an Egk man now or Egk's men were just ordinary fellows when not on duty. Martin wanted to be able to say that it was too dangerous to take action, and that Oser and Egk should be given the benefit of the doubt because it was too soon after the elections. He did not see these as contradictory positions. Just then the tennis ball soared out of the field and bounced past Uwe Wurfel, still seated by the teapots. Two fieldsmen ran after the ball and one of them, without breaking his stride, pushed Uwe off the stool. Martin began to run. On the playing field men rollicked in the grass. By the time Martin reached the camp fire Uwe Wurfel was being helped to his feet by Lieutenant Dinham, who had been lighting a cigarette with a coal. 'Not too popular, are we?' he was saying.

'I'll help him now,' said Martin.

Uwe Wurfel was panting. Martin helped him undo the top button on his shirt.

'He's always getting into strife,' said Dinham. 'What's going on, that's what I'd like to know. Something is, and when something's going on in my camp I like to get to the bottom of it.' He peered into Uwe's face. 'Is this joker a Nazi or what? That's why the others are always knocking him around, isn't it.'

'He's not a Nazi. They're the Nazis,' said Martin.

'I don't like it,' said Dinham. He pointed the damp end of his cigarette at Martin. 'I remember you. That day at the gate. In my camp people keep their noses clean.'

He walked away.

'Now we're Nazis,' said Martin. 'Did you hear what he said?'

But Uwe Wurfel was making the tea again.

'If you can't help yourself I can't help you,' shouted Martin. He was glad when the order was given to pack up.

To avoid passing through Tatura the lorries used back roads. The sun was beginning to go down and the internees, exposed to the cooling air, turned up their collars and stared at the reddening horizon. The camp commandant was waiting for them on his office verandah in the military compound, smiling around his pipe like a solicitous uncle. He knocked the pipe bowl against a post and hurried down the steps, crying, 'Welcome back, welcome back, how did it go?'

Dr Oser and Lieutenant Dinham met him as he crossed the yard, shook his hand, murmured to him.

'Oh dear,' said the commandant. 'Oh dear, oh dear, oh dear.'

After a while he walked among the internees, his empty pipe in his teeth, apologizing, asking them if they were all right, asking them if they had enjoyed the picnic at least. 'Yes,' they said. 'Thank you.' He said 'Dreadful' once or twice and got in the way when they unloaded the lorries.

A time bell clanged. Lights began to go on in the buildings and along the perimeter fence, and the new watch climbed the towers and turned on the searchlights. In the military compound the internees finished unloading the lorries and waited for

57

Lieutenant Dinham's guards to escort them through the gates. Martin and Professor Steiner stood at either end of the trestle table, while other men held pots, cane baskets and bundles of rubbish. 'Hurry up,' one man said. Everything out here was unfamiliar, even precarious, and the dinner bugle had just sounded.

The guards opened the gates and Lieutenant Dinham counted the internees as they filed past him into the prison compound. Here they lined up again; they knew the procedure by now. But at the moment the last man was counted the Lieutenant commanded, 'Nobody move. We're one short.'

He backed into the military compound, blowing his whistle and looking up at the watchtowers. 'Lights! Over here, quick about it.'

He peered at shapes in the twilight. When the searchlights swung round he opened his holster flap.

'He's here somewhere,' he said. 'I'll get the bastard.'

A number of guards with rifles joined him.

'All right, spread out. He can't have gone far.'

'Should we perhaps count the men again, Lieutenant?'

But Lieutenant Dinham might not have heard his commanding officer. He drew his revolver and loped, half-crouched to take the enemy, down the path next to the telegraph hut. Searchlights led the other guards between the gloomy lorries, behind the officers' mess, to the main gates and back again.

'Oy,' said a man in a tower. 'In the truck there, look.'

His searchlight quivered. Uwe Wurfel, as small as a child waiting outside a saloon bar, was forced to avert his eyes.

'Out you come,' said a guard, opening the door.

'I might have known,' said Lieutenant Dinham. He reached into the cabin of the lorry.

The internees saw Uwe Wurfel pitch against the door as he fell. A number of them cried out, 'Buffalo Bill,' again and again, with increasing venom, as the prisoner was cuffed towards them.

'Steady on, Lieutenant. That will do,' said the commandant.

'He's a troublemaker, sir. This isn't the first time.'

'Then you'd better take him to the bunker, I suppose. We'll decide the sentence in the morning.'

'Yes, sir.'

The internees continued to jostle and cry out, held back from the gates by the tiny coaxing motions of a line of bayonet tips. But the pushing and shoving stopped only when the red berets had manoeuvred Martin and certain other men into isolated positions. Martin understood that he should say and do nothing.

# CHAPTER 13

First he stripped his bunk of sheets and blankets, folded and stacked them with his pillow, and carried the bedding to the gardeners' hut. On his next trip he moved all his clothes, books and odds and ends in his suitcase. He went back then for his palliasse. Like any old mattress it was innocently stained; Martin remembered the day he and the children spring-cleaned the house, Paul snortling, Nina telling him red-faced to stop it. He rolled up the palliasse, took it to the gardeners' hut, and went back for the bed frame. The red beret supervising him did not offer to help.

Other space was available here and there in the camp but Martin had had enough of endless war talk and sad cases and listening to men who took you aside confidentially. He did not want to move into the schoolhut and wait for Uwe Wurfel's return. He did not want to live with other exiles in the entertainment hall storeroom. He had his stencil plates, his diary, and his garden – larger now than anyone else's – and that was enough. He looked forward to making the gardeners' hut habitable.

The rakes, spades, hoes, dusting powders, buckets, coils of hose, tins of tap washers and sacks of fowl manure he stacked against an outside wall until he had scrounged enough leftover building material to make a small lean-to shelter, with shelves, in which to store it all. Now and then another gardener might clatter a spade handle against the wall while he was resting, but that wouldn't matter. He swept out the hut, sealed the holes in the walls, and laid an old carpet on the floor. He lined the walls with empty washed manure sacks sewn together and hung with stencils. It was almost always cold in the hut but lining the walls helped, and by the end of May he had made himself a brazier in the workshop. He used candles and a small oil lantern at night.

He washed the dusty windows and soaped oil and grease off the table underneath it, creating for himself a broad, well-lit workbench for his stencil making. To transform the hard-featured outside walls he trained a morning glory vine along bits and pieces of wire and wooden laths he found in the dump behind the workshop. He encouraged a lima bean plant around the door frame.

In the mornings he weeded, planted seeds according to the season, dug small drainage channels and helped other internees with their gardens. He cut stencils in the afternoons. He had the time now to please himself: he had few customers anymore because he was marked. The shapes in his new pictures were those a searchlight reveals. In the evenings he added to his diary, writing in the central pages of the ledger-book. He did not, as such, write about the ascension of stealth, goading and resettlement as the camp's way of life, but used them to make philosophical reflections and observations of behaviour. He ignored the case notes at the beginning and end of the ledger-book and believed that he might tear them out one day. Letters arrived from home; nothing in them compelled him to take them apart. He stopped attending lectures because rarely could he find a lecturer who did not invoke the Party in some way, but from time to time he visited the library, intending to start on the works of the important thinkers. All in all he felt imperturbable, contemplative; his life had the configuration of happiness.

Uwe Wurfel endured the bunker for the second time and returned to the camp a little paler from the lack of sunlight but otherwise unchanged. He paced the camp boundary three or four times a day. He no longer worked with the Empire Builders. It was pointless trying to converse with him. Yet, at the same time, you would not quite say that he was destroyed or forlorn or adrift. It was Martin's belief that Uwe Wurfel's disengagement was simply an unsatisfactory version of his own.

A few friends and fellow exiles came by now and then, including Professor Steiner who sometimes managed to evade the red berets stationed outside his quarters in the entertainment hall storeroom. The visitors usually brought pastries with them. Martin made tea or coffee unless he had been unable to barter for any. If there were no other visitors Professor Steiner spoke about resistance. Martin spoke about books. No one expected the visits would be allowed to continue. Martin could not say, 'I don't want you to come anymore', but he hoped there would be no incidents.

On the twentieth of June there was another festival, celebrating fertility in Europe with the sun's return from the Tropic of Capricorn. Martin spent the sunless day in his hut, cutting stencils and reading. He did not trouble to go to the sportsground that evening, but he could see the glow of the bonfires from his window. He took note of the silhouettes.

As the banishments and assaults continued, the number of escape attempts grew. One man was found clinging to the chassis of the mail van. Another broke away from the road-making crew but was captured by police at the railway station that afternoon. Three men discovered a blind spot in the perimeter fence, cut the wire, and ran, crouching, to the pine trees at the farm bordering with the camp. Two of them were brought back under guard the next day and given twenty-one days solitary confinement. Police arrested the third man a month later after tracing him to the German community in the Barossa Valley: consequently the attorney-general signed a number of new internment orders. The cry *Haussuchung* was commonly heard. Buffalo Bill's men found loose floorboards in several huts, a loose cement block in the laundry, and ten feet of excavation under the bootmaker's hut. The bootmaker refused to say who had been digging there and was given seven days in the bunker. They searched Martin's hut nine times in July and August. 'Acting on information received,' Lieutenant Dinham would say. 'This wouldn't be tunnel dirt, by any chance?' he would say, kicking at something in Martin's garden. As Martin expected, the raids discouraged his visitors.

One day in September, Professor Steiner knocked on his door, his first visit for many weeks.

'Even our red-capped friends don't like to stand about in the rain,' the professor explained. 'As a result, I have been everywhere this morning. May I . . .?'

He shook the water off his coat and hung it on Martin's door. Coins jingled in the pockets. His boots and trousers were sodden and splashed with mud. He brushed the water droplets from his beard.

'Sit down and warm your hands,' said Martin.

The professor pulled the work stool out from under the bench and sat next to Martin by the brazier. 'You have the most agreeable quarters in the camp,' he said, holding his palms close to the red coals. Now and then he plucked at the knees and thighs of his damp trousers.

'Unfortunately I have only a coffee substitute,' said Martin. 'The taste is abominable. Or there is tea made from herbs. I made it myself. It's not so bad.'

'Tea please,' said the professor.

Martin made the tea in a pot that he had bought at a May Day stall.

'Also no sugar,' he said.

Professor Steiner shrugged. 'And I did not bring any pastries, so I cannot complain.'

'How are things in the storeroom?'

'Joseph Canzler was thrown out of Hut 14 last Friday, so he is with us for the time being. It is getting crowded.'

'They should build us more huts,' said Martin.

'Do they even know?' Professor Steiner gestured, spilling his tea. 'The commandant thinks we are all alike here behind the wire. He thinks it is natural and harmless if we fly the flag and celebrate our Fuehrer's birthday. On Saturday evening he has Oser to dinner. He offers him wine. If I may employ an Australian expression, *he wouldn't have a clue*.'

They looked at the dim coals. Martin said, 'You said you have been everywhere this morning. What have you been doing?'

Professor Steiner took a newspaper clipping from his shirt pocket and gave it to Martin. 'We are collecting money for Russia.'

The newspaper item explained how the beleaguered people of

Russia might be helped by donations to the Red Cross. Farmers had pledged sheepskins for coats. Brisbane schoolchildren had knitted a quantity of scarves. Money and old clothes were needed.

'The banking officer has agreed to exchange our tokens,' said the professor. 'Anything you can spare will be most welcome.'

'Oser and Egk won't like this,' said Martin.

'We won't ask them.'

'That's not what I meant,' said Martin. He gave a mixture of brass and copper tokens to the professor, who put them into his pocket.

'We shall see.'

Professor Steiner stopped for a second cup of tea. By lunchtime the rain had stopped and in the afternoon Martin inspected his garden for rain damage. There was also a leak in his roof.

At half past three he walked across to the post office hut. It was still closed, and dozens of internees stood irresolute on the muddy path. The mail van would be twenty minutes late, someone said. Apparently a creek was in flood somewhere. Should they wait? Or was there time for a cup of tea.

They were diverted by the arrival of Professor Steiner and four other men, who began walking among them, shaking cotton drawstring purses. The professor wore a cardboard badge. He went from man to man, explaining, sometimes debating. He was obliged to raise his voice.

But men began to give him coins, and others asked questions. They were from the camp's heartland, from the mass which could let itself be turned by ceremonies. In the mess hall and on the parade ground there were always hard eyes upon them, but here they felt unnoticed because of the mud, the crowd and their common need of a letter from home.

And perhaps many of them felt that it was time. When someone jostled the professor, a number of men retaliated at once, and they all heaved and surged on the path. Martin's dejection lifted away. He began reaching like a child in an orchard, one hand snatching at the air. Then he roared, a red beret tight in his fingers. Around him pairs of men struggled and fell in the mud. Martin laughed. He sought the professor, flapping the beret before his face. 'Look!'

The resistance spread to most areas of the compound. Knots of internees plunged among the camp buildings, seeking sensations and enemies. Men stood outside every hut, shouting insults and encouragement; others trailed at a half-run behind the fighting. Martin followed them, witnessing victories, which he described at intervals to the professor at the post office hut.

'Egk is down,' he panted.

Egk had been backed against a water tank. His face was full of hate. He named his oppressors, taunted them, and they threw him down. He was kicked, turned over like a boneless creature in the mud.

'We've won,' said Martin.

Every hut-leader had been ejected, knocked to the ground with his clothes and palliasse. Dr Oser fled to the main gate as internees fought through to his office. They heaped his papers on the floor and called for matches. Martin had found himself prancing at the edge of the hasty fire, kicking awkwardly at the heavy scorched bundles.

'Oser is finished,' he told the professor.

Others took up this cry. Professor Steiner's supporters, so swift and exultant, now held the camp. They stood about, tired and surprised. They had no plans; no leaders had been declared. They had no weapons. They were thinly placed, only two or three men here and there, after all, but they claimed victory.

And so the battle turned. The professor's supporters panted and laughed when other men might have known to follow through. From hidden places between the huts the red berets uncovered razors and nailed clubs and planks, and emerged with them, mute, solemn, thorough.

'Herr Linke,' one man said. He motioned with an old kitchen knife.

Martin drew back with a slap against a door. The blade was rusty, honed to a wisp, barely useful, but it had come from nowhere, and seemed to him cruel and slippery.

He had been building upon sand; everything was an accident. He closed his arms around his stomach, side-stepped away, and began to run. Two men ran by him and once he heard cries of pain. The sounds of battle were cries and running footsteps. Behind the post office hut he found the professor, sheltering with other men among empty crates. He huddled with them and listened. Up in the towers the sentries wound the siren handles.

A short time later guards streamed into the camp from the military compound.

'I think it's safe now,' said Martin. He had been trembling.

Professor Steiner stepped away from the wall. 'But what now?' he demanded. He looked in irritation at his cotton purse of coins and handed it to another man.

Two guards, running with their rifles held against their chests, rounded the corner of the hut. 'Assembly ground,' they said. 'Quick.'

Guards moved from hut to hut in the compound, pulling out the internees and force marching them to the assembly ground. They scraped the toes of their boots against the men's ankles and bruised their spines with rifle punches. The watchtower guards threw their cigarettes away. The sirens whined. On the assembly ground the internees were ringed by guards, who whispered to them: 'Come on, Fritz. Come on.'

Professor Steiner pulled Martin's sleeve. 'Something is happening,' he said, beginning to push men aside.

Martin followed him through to the inner edge of the crowd, where internees were shouting over the shoulders of the guards who held them back. On an area of ground a doctor and two nurses were crouched next to men with razor-slash wounds. Lieutenant Dinham and the camp commandant were watching guards search Dr Oser, Theodor Egk and several of the red berets, who stood scowling in a line, their hands clasped on their heads. Dr Oser was white-faced, hot-eyed, as though about to rush and bite. The commandant stepped back from him, looking shocked. 'Albert,' he said. Theodor Egk tweaked his head in a spasm of pain, he swayed and fell to the ground, and he lay there spitting and hawking to rid his nose and mouth of blood. The internees jeered when Lieutenant Dinham pulled him to his feet, and they hooted and whistled when he went along the line of prisoners seizing berets. He dropped the berets onto a pile of planks, bricks and sharpened metal weapons. Taking his pipe away from his mouth, the commandant peered down at the berets and doubtfully prodded them with the toe cap of his shoe.

'I believe it's over, Martin,' Professor Steiner said.

For a moment Martin misunderstood the professor. The change seemed important enough to signal everyone's freedom.

# CHAPTER 14

The new camp commandant was a short, hearty man who watched, his hands on his hips, as changes were made. He appointed Professor Steiner camp-leader, sent Dr Oser to another camp, and pulled down the swastikas. With Professor Steiner's help, he identified and broke up the old concentrations of party sympathizers, and banned the red berets. All this happened within four days.

On a windy day at the end of the week he called the internees to an assembly. Professor Steiner and Lieutenant Dinham stood with him on the platform.

'As you well know,' he said immediately, 'things have not been very satisfactory in this camp. Some of you have been persecuted, others have been influenced by Nazi fanatics. All that's got to stop. There have been too many escapes and escape attempts. These must also stop.' He looked at Lieutenant Dinham and then at the internees again, and said, more amiably, 'Many of you are overdue for release anyhow. Starting from next Monday, any man who wants his case heard by the appeals tribunal can come and see me and we'll make the necessary arrangements. It will be slow, so be warned. Now,' he said, 'you all know Professor Steiner.' He inclined his head to the professor, who put his hands behind his back. 'I understand he's been the voice of reason here. I'm relying on you to help him help me.'

The fellow's reforms had been hard and fast. They promised upheaval and made Martin apprehensive. But here was sympathy, and Martin, clapping with the other internees, was reminded of Major Orr in Liverpool.

'There you are,' said Professor Steiner in the mess hall at lunchtime. He sat down next to Martin.

'You must be pleased,' said Martin.

'Thank you, I am,' said the professor. 'He's a fair man. He's *cluey*, as they say.'

'Did he send Egk away too?'

'Egk? No, Egk is still in hospital.'

A number of internees walked by their table during the meal, stopping to congratulate the professor. Some of them seemed furtive and confiding: these were not mannerisms that could be discarded overnight.

'You're a popular man,' said Martin.

The professor negligently waved his fork. When he had finished eating, he turned side on in his chair and cocked his head. 'We must not forget you, of course,' he said, poking Martin in the shoulder.

Martin waited, saying nothing.

'Your appeal,' said the professor. 'We'll have to see what we can do about it.'

'I must admit that I was encouraged by the commandant's remarks,' said Martin.

'Shall we approach him together, you and I? I will give him a favourable account of your conduct. Who knows, it may reach the ears of the judges.'

Martin traced the wood grain on the table top with his forefinger. 'I don't know. Will it harm me, this unorthodox approach?'

'This is not the time for scruples, my friend,' said the professor. He paused. 'But do not think I will be other than truthful.'

'Of course not, of course not,' said Martin. 'Please, I did not mean to suggest that.'

'I will simply tell him that you resisted Egk and Oser, that you were a victim. No more, no less.'

'Yes. Thank you. I understand,' said Martin.

Professor Steiner took a cigarette packet from his pocket and weighed it in his palm. 'From the commandant. Do you know the expression they use for these? Tailor made.'

'I must go,' said Martin. 'There is a small queue gathering to see you.'

'I will need good men, Martin,' the professor said.

Martin sat down again.

'For a committee. I will need good men close to me. I can offer accommodation in Oser's old quarters. Very comfortable.'

But Martin saw men putting on their clothes or coughing in the mornings, the film from their breathing on the cold iron walls, his stencils and plates cramped and creased in boxes under his bunk. His life was bare, but he feared any change.

'I would be no good at that,' he said. 'I would be no good on a committee. I am sorry, I couldn't.'

He wanted to say that he would be released sooner or later because a year had gone by. Why, I don't even mean the red berets any harm, he wanted to say. Where the other fellows cause them to flinch and skulk in the mess, I let them be. 'I couldn't,' he said.

'A pity,' said the professor. 'If that is your answer then I had better let you get back to work.'

'But thank you,' said Martin. 'The other matter? You will make an appointment and let me know?'

'If you wish.'

Still speaking rapidly, Martin said, 'And Uwe Wurfel? Perhaps we can help him too?'

Professor Steiner looked at him and said, 'Don't you think you should stop now, while you are ahead?'

Martin went immediately to his garden and duplicated the tasks on which he had worked that morning. At half past three he was one of the first internees to gather outside the post office hut. That left three more diversions in the day: a chat with friends after work, dinner, the slide lecture on India by some visitor.

There was a letter for him, from Jean, describing certain developments. 'With all the men Manpowered or in the army,' she wrote, 'there's no one around to do the farm work. Hartley can't get the time off, as you know, Martin, and it's too big a job for one man.' She explained that the young fellows appointed to carry out the conversion of Martin's farm had gone into the army or something, and that was why three Italian prisoners-of-war were now living in the barn and a manager was in Nina's sleepout bedroom, boarding with the widow from the cannery. 'It's wonderful what they're capable of. One of them cemented up the steps to the front verandah and fixed the tank stand. All three have got green fingers, so everything's coming along nicely. Hartley says to tell you they've fixed that problem with the ignition on the tractor. We pop in on the weekends to check on things, but the manager seems reliable and they have to report regularly. They're good with the children, too, which is a blessing, teaching them to play soccer and what have you.'

While I live in a concentration camp, thought Martin. While I get mud on my boots and clothes like a common peasant and the peasants are free to frolic in my garden and look in perversion at my children and maybe take them behind the barn. He wrote these things in both sets of case-notes in his ledger-book. He told himself not to blunder and be rash next time he saw the professor. He hadn't the interest to write in his diary.

Martin spent the following days filling the time-gulfs with unread books and unsatisfactory stencils. At mealtimes he watched Professor Steiner eating with his committee members or mingling with the internees. They were days of expectation and doubt, until the evening Professor Steiner paused at his table, spoke encouragingly to several men, and said, before he drifted on: 'Your appointment is listed on the notice board, Martin.'

Dozens of names, with quarter-hour intervals between the appointment times. Martin noted that he was down for a quarter past three the next afternoon. He absorbed little of the evening's concert but told himself not to anticipate anything, or even open the ledger-book. In the mess the next day he was serene; his hand was precise on his stencil plates. To thank the professor he nodded and smiled from a distance, knowing to leave it at that: the professor, though generous, was clearly very busy, and Martin had been a disappointment to him.

Feeling composed and tolerant, Martin left early for his appointment and visited Uwe Wurfel in the schoolhut. Wurfel was in bed, awake but hunched beneath many blankets. His unwashed clothes lay with dusty fluff-balls on the floor; knuckles

71

of breadcrusts and an apple core on the bedside chair stopped Martin from sitting down. There was no other furniture, and no pictures hung on the walls. One visible eye watched Martin from the bed. Martin breathed shallowly of air stale and now nervy with Wurfel's unfathomable emotions. Did he even know about the changes?

'Are you cold? Shall I fetch you more blankets?'

Wurfel did not answer, his silence causing Martin to say too much of little account, just as it always had. In his shame, Martin recognized the self interest behind his errand. He walked to the door, but turned around.

'Look,' he said. 'I will say this: now is the time to ask the tribunal to review your position. You said once you would wait for the tide to turn? It has. And I believe you know everything that is going on.'

That restored him, and the first thing he said to the commandant in his office was: 'Perhaps you know Major Orr of the Liverpool camp? He was a great help at the time of my first appeal.'

'Orr? Yes, I do.' The commandant laughed, still clasping and periodically shaking Martin's hand. 'They give all the old duffers these jobs, you know.' He had been wounded in Crete. 'Here,' he said, releasing Martin's hand to touch his upper arm, 'and here.' He pounded his thigh. 'Your blokes really had me in their sights that day. Have a seat.' His laughter and speech were like barks and shouts.

Martin felt sufficiently encouraged to say: 'Not my blokes at all. I have lived in Australia for seventeen years now.'

'Quite right.' The commandant opened Martin's file and began to read. He said 'mm hm' and 'yes' and 'right', turning the loose sheets and stapled reports as though tearing them from a pad. He looked up. 'You've appealed before.'

Did he not listen? 'Many of us have,' said Martin.

'Oh.' The commandant continued to read.

'I believe Professor Steiner told you about me?'

'Sound, that Steiner. Very sound. You're lucky to have him. Here we are.' The commandant held up a small sheet of paper.

' "Unsympathetic to Oser's regime". Odd way of putting it. "Unsympathetic to Oser's regime. Was among those banished and forced to seek other quarters". Settled in again all right, have you?'

'Settled in?'

'Back in the fold again,' said the commandant.

'I converted the gardeners' hut,' said Martin. 'I'm quite happy there.'

'You're not in one of the dormitory huts?'

'I don't mind being alone,' said Martin.

The commandant closed the file. 'That's not the point. It's security. I can't have fellows living by themselves all over the place. It weakens security. Who else is there? Why didn't Steiner tell me this? Why didn't Dinham, for that matter.'

The commandant continued to think aloud. Martin's heart pounded.

'Soon we'll have every Tom, Dick and Harry wanting his own hut. Who else is there?'

Martin told him about Uwe Wurfel in the spare room of the schoolhut. 'But he's difficult. No one can converse with him. Whatever you do with me,' said Martin, to remind the commandant, 'Uwe Wurfel should be allowed to go home. He'll get well again if he's allowed to go home.'

'He'll have to move back into a proper hut first,' said the commandant, writing in a notebook next to his telephone. 'I'll see what Steiner says. And I want you to see my clerk about another hut for yourself. As for your appeal,' he passed a form to Martin, 'fill this in and give it to my clerk.'

Martin picked up and looked at the form and made a gesture of powerlessness. 'I did all this a year ago,' he said. 'Do you think I stand a chance?'

'Might. Might not. They're not as tough as they were.' He tapped Martin's file. 'You've been behaving yourself, haven't you?'

'Professor Steiner's report,' said Martin. 'I was one of those who stood up to Oser.' My God, he thought.

'Got you now,' said the commandant, putting his hand to his forehead.

73

'You see,' said Martin, 'how can they keep me in here and let Italian war prisoners live in freedom and luxury on my farm. Can you give me an answer to that, I wonder.'

The commandant patted files and papers into order on his desk. 'I don't know anything about that,' he said. 'Out of my jurisdiction. Perhaps you'll be home soon to deal with it. Anything else? Tell the next bloke he can come in now. All righty?'

This time his handshake, like his manner of speaking and laughing, was brisk and hard.

The commandant's clerk told Martin to move into Hut 11. If you think I am moving right here and now you are mistaken, thought Martin. His dissenting thoughts sustained him until he reached the hut in the garden and lay upon his bed.

The next morning he sought the hut-leader of Hut 11, to advise him that he would be moving in: 'Sooner or later,' he would tell the fellow. At first he thought no one was inside the hut; the sheet-folds and blankets were as tight as drums on every bunk, the air was torpid, and some of his stencils – he could not look at them – had been pinned to the walls. Just as he was asking himself how could he go back to all this, he saw that a man, propped on his elbows, was watching him from a corner bunk.

'You're back,' said Martin.

'There is no one here,' said Theodor Egk. 'You may hit and kick me quite openly. Or is it to be sodomy? Are you the first in line this morning, Herr Linke? Is your retarded friend also here?'

The conspicuous bruises around Egk's eyes were like shadows. Martin drew closer and saw Egk's derisive expression and the stitches along one eyebrow.

'If I did you would deserve it,' he said. He was fascinated. He peered at Egk. 'Request a transfer to another camp,' he said.

Egk lay back. 'You don't know anything. Where is the punishment in that? Steiner is relying on you all.'

They were interrupted by the hut-leader. 'You may have the bunk next to our friend here,' he told Martin.

'It may be four or five days before I can move my things,' said Martin.

At no time did the hut-leader look away from Egk. 'We'll save you a piece of him,' the hut-leader said.

Martin delayed for three days. He might have delayed longer but for Professor Steiner visiting him and saying: 'We would like you to participate in the Harvest Thanksgiving displays on the first of October.' He asked if Martin had thought further about joining the committee. 'Then I expect you will be moving hut soon,' the professor said, looking around at the walls and ceiling of the gardeners' hut. Martin took his things out after lunch.

He did not know what the men of Hut 11 did to Egk in the darkness, but that afternoon Egk was locked in the bunker after having stunned a guard and run naked up and down the perimeter fence, cursing and waving the guard's rifle. One evening after roll call a week later, Egk appeared in the hut doorway. He hesitated, gauging the treacherous stretches of floorboards to his bunk. As Martin watched, he passed through the room, and settled beneath the blankets on his bunk. He slept: Martin heard him toss and mutter. No one crossed to his bunk in the night. The men had lost interest in him.

By day Egk could be seen, arms swinging, striding across the compound. Often he hesitated and frowned after a short distance, as though he had just remembered something. Sometimes he was greeted by a camp cat, a contemptuous round-faced tom with torn grey ears which he fed with kitchen scraps after every meal, clapping his hands at the other strays. Egk was like Uwe Wurfel, possessed of directionless energy, and often when one paced the perimeter fence the other followed, unnoticed and unnoticing.

Like Wurfel before him, Egk beat futilely against inclosure. Again he was sent to the bunker, this time for walking through the gate left open for the mail van. Guards called on him to stop, but he kept walking, without hurry, and Lieutenant Dinham took up a rifle and led the shooting. Martin saw it and shouted disgustedly: 'Buffalo Bill.' The guards fired eighteen shots, into the air above Egk's head and into the ground at his feet. They might have wanted to see him dance. Egk, his clothes flapping, stood as still as a man who has seen a snake cross his path.

Then one day in the mess Egk took his bread roll and plate of stew to where Uwe Wurfel was sitting. The men at the next table put down their knives and forks expectantly but, without looking up, Wurfel made room for Egk. After that the two men ate together, walked together, two bony unquiet men with glittering eyes and lips that were never still. And one night Egk leaned into the gap separating his bunk from Martin's and began to whisper.

# CHAPTER 15

'I attacked people with iron bars, Martin, communist workers and intellectuals at their rallies. I threw bricks through the windows of Jewish shops. I cut off the hair and beards of devout Jews and let the scissors slip and the skin pull away with the hair. We ruled the streets like wild natives. Blood ran, Martin.'

'I'm not interested,' Martin said. He said it every night. "I'm tired. Tell someone else.'

'But anyone can break bones and wipe the blood from his fingers. We all did it; we did not think about it. Now I do, of course.'

A voice from another bunk would shout *shut up*, and Egk would subside, but softly through the dark would come his whisper again:

'There are worse things. It is a worse thing to parade a human variation and call it an imperfection. Do you understand what I am saying, Martin? Yet I was very good at it.'

Every night Egk whispered, and every day he walked shoulder to shoulder around the compound with Uwe Wurfel, always moving on to avoid the taunts and sly blows and thrown stones. Did he confess then, too? Egk's voice – the precise quality of his whisper – and the little mattress creaks as he raised himself on his elbow and leaned into the darkness, stole into Martin's mind. To the meaning of Egk's words he paid no attention. He waited for the long days to finish, and waited for sleep, hearing always the phantom and then the actual voice of Theodor Egk. 'Leave me alone,' Martin said, tossing in his bunk, and a sleeping man nearby might wake and cry, 'Won't you be quiet?' and fists might strike them in the dark.

At the end of October officials came to the camp and heard the appeals. 'Owing to the fact of your hearing in 1942, Mr Linke,' they said, 'we shall dispense with some of the formalities.' The earlier evidence would stand, they said: all they needed to do now was review it in the light of his activities since then. They had files and reports before them. Martin Paul Linke had worked on a now-banned camp newspaper; he manufactured and distributed pictures of a pro-German nature; he was a friend of the internee Uwe Wurfel, known for his troublesome behaviour and escape attempts; in recent weeks he had entered into an association with the Nazi, Theodor Egk. Under Section 26 of the National Security Regulations, they said, they could not recommend the release of the internee Martin Paul Linke.

Egk whispered, 'Martin, do you understand what I am saying? In the Strassergarten I stripped the homosexuals naked and painted their organs pink. I hacked the beards off the old Jews and forced the communists to eat their own pamphlets. I humiliated Herr Wurfel all those months, and I humiliated you as well. I was twisted up with plotting and treachery.' Someone threw a boot at them. 'But now there is one picture stronger than any of these,' Egk whispered.

'Let me sleep, let me think,' Martin moaned.

They had all dangled 'one year' under his nose to keep him happy. They should not have said anything. He should not have listened. He had been like the convict who learns to manage time because he knows his release date. But no, he is an internee; he might be freed tomorrow, or never, or five years from now. Late or never, he thought; not tomorrow. The passing weeks, therefore, do not lead to anything, and the passing hours are marked only by meals and lights-out and the arrival of the mail van.

Soon Martin could not finish a book, he cut no new stencil plates, and one hour bent over his plants was more than enough. In his dreams he was always hungry and lived in shame: he asked if he might eat another man's leftovers; he huddled over thick damp chocolate cakes, pastry cornets, tarts, fruit pies and bowls of scalded cream, dabbing at every flake and crumb with an undignified wet finger and wanting more; and when he awoke he found it was true. He spent all his tokens buying pastries from

78

the pastrycook hut or scarcities and luxuries from wealthy internees and the men who received food parcels. He ate two pastries with morning coffee, two after lunch and two with afternoon tea. He took pastries along when he attended the evening concerts and slide lectures. No one else ate so many pastries. In the mess line he estimated his neighbours' serves with his practised eye, measuring luck or unfairness in mouthfuls. It hurt him to see someone get the choice portions. 'Here, here, here, here, here,' said the men at his table one day, offering him their unwanted scraps, which he swallowed, averting his hot face. Martin gorged; he felt large and soft but still hungry. He spent all his tokens and, needing more, sold his tobacco allowance to a higher bidder and the products of his garden to the inmates, the mess cooks, the guards in the garrison. He found new buyers for his stencils. Like a counterfeiter printing bank notes, Martin printed fresh currency with his stencil plates. He got no joy from it.

'In Kenya, Martin, I had black servants. You can imagine what that meant for a man such as I had become. I was there to sow discord and buy influence and spies among the Arab traders and shopkeepers. We had a natural affinity, me with my despised black servants, they with their slave-master pasts. My government chose well, Martin.' Egk said softly, 'A shame about your appeal, Martin.'

At night when the lights were turned off he had nothing to avail his weakness, the darkness or Egk's insinuating whisper. At night the perimeter fence contracted, drawing the barbed wire right up to the walls of the hut. He heard the scratching but he was bound to his bunk by Egk's confidences. Men coughed in the mornings and revealed their careless habits, and Martin lay and counted the hours until he might again sleep.

'All those things, Martin. But there is one that will not let me alone now. Martin,' Egk might whisper, 'do you know how to drive a car?'

Martin kept his wristwatch in his shirt pocket because the leather strap was friable. He took it out a hundred times a day,

79

straining and eventually tearing the pockets of his shirts, but he registered only how slow an hour was. He bought cotton thread and a needle at the canteen and mended his pockets. Small actions like this used up time; he planned for one each day, and felt disordered if he could not think of one. He had to buy more thread, and demonstrated to the man in the canteen how it was he damaged his pockets. 'Why don't you buy a watch strap from Max Hirtreiter,' the man said, but Martin said no, someone had stolen his boots the moment he arrived here and no doubt the leather had found its way to Hirtreiter. He did not say that he also needed the sewing time and could not afford to spend the tokens. Seated on his bunk later with his sewing gear he thought: My contracted life will fit upon this needle point. He dragged out his watch; the hands disclosed that it was still far too early to go to the post office hut.

'We were making a film, you understand, an instructional film. Very scientific and serious, oh yes, with a "professor" to explain the evidence. I think you will understand me when I say these "professors" were always presentable older men who wore glasses, spoke convincingly, and happened to be between roles at the moment. We took the tram, Martin, we went by tram to commit outrage, buying tickets and ringing the bell like everyone else. The other passengers knew something was up, of course, and sat stiff and afraid. We got off at the platz on Wilhelmstrasse, where the little tables and chairs sit on the footpath outside the cafes and delicatessens. It was a Sunday and we could be sure of a crowd of them: lovers sitting under the yellow umbrellas, families meeting, everyone talking at once, that kind of thing. It can be irritating to watch. I marched in, taking my time to get a good look at all the faces, going from one end of the platz to the other, and on the way back I pointed and said, "that one", "that one", and my men grabbed and held them until we were ready to start filming. I selected a range of types. A child with rickets, I remember. The usual old man wearing the black hat and coat. I expect he shuffled and had that unreadable conformity that used to get me down. Yes, a gypsy child begging, quite filthy, but she gave us the slip. A Serb. You've seen Serbs, you know what I'm talking about. Oh, everybody: I knew what the producer wanted and it was someone else's job to write the "professor's" commentary. So, we had a good selection and proceeded to film them. This depended on what it was about them. Some we made walk up and down the path by the fountain, that way we had their shops in the background, others we made sit on the low barrier that goes round the fountain. That's fine, they were scared or sullen but we filmed them. Now I was never in these films, you understand, but I did have to demonstrate, so to speak, and the voice of the "professor" did the rest. All you saw was my arm and the riding crop I always carried. So, the subject is sitting on the wall, the camera is focussed and beginning to film, and I push and poke the head this way and that with the riding crop to show the shape of the nose and brow, the head size, the position of the eyes, the hairline, that kind of thing. It gave me mad satisfaction.

'But there was a woman, she was I suppose in her thirties with a scarf around her head. That's why I chose her, she looked as though she'd come straight from the cow bails to the big city for the day. Without the scarf she was neither one thing nor the other, but we went ahead and I started tapping her cheeks with my little whip. Now, unlike the others she kept jerking away from me so she could face the camera and smile. She had dimples, it was a glorious smile. Why did she smile? Especially in the light of what happened next, when she put her hand to her mouth like a blushing girl and I pulled it away just in time to see that she had metal teeth the colour of lead in her mouth. I held her lips open. That is the thing I think of now. Martin,' Egk would whisper, 'did you know that there is a place on the perimeter fence where the searchlights do not converge?'

Among the camp cats there was one that Martin liked to scoop from the ground and rock in his arms. Often, with little cries, it trotted out from under the mess to slope and flex around his legs. 'You faithless creature,' said Martin in the voice the loveless men used for the camp animals. He patted Sergeant Loman's dog, watched the waterbirds and scattered crumbs for the sparrows. On the day the letter came he embraced a horse, held himself tight against an old draught horse that had brought in a wagonload of fowl manure from one of the farms. While the farmer stood on the wagon tray shovelling the manure into a stall alongside the gardeners' hut, Martin whispered to the horse, his head laid against the tremors in its soft neck. 'Goodbye,' he said, when the farmer drove away. 'Thank you.' He walked to the post office hut, where he was handed a letter from Jean.

'Listen to me,' he said later. 'You listen to me, now.'

He had searched the compound until he found Egk walking with Wurfel on the sportsground. Someone had thrown mud at them. They seemed unsurprised to see him, nodding as if they had expected it but not wanted to precipitate it.

'You listen to me, now,' Martin said. 'She wants them, she doesn't want them, she wants them, she doesn't want them. Now she wants them.' He held the letter up and said, in a falsetto voice: '*She is their mother, after all. We think it's a real shame they never see their Dad or their Mum*. The courts decided who should see them but that means nothing to some people, it seems. *She lives by herself in town these days*. Oh sure; she's knocking with the Italian war prisoners and thinking she can take away my farm. *It's only for weekends*. That's enough time to fill their heads with lies.'

Oh yes, they understood.

Twice a day the three men circled the compound. 'The thing is, Martin,' Egk would say, 'Uwe does not drive and I might make an error.' 'The guards are not so vigilant at night,' he would say. At a certain point on the perimeter fence he would say, 'This is the place I was talking about.'

# PART THREE

# CHAPTER 16

Egk had plans in his head and a map in his pocket and he possessed all the intelligence once gathered by Dr Oser's escape committee. He had even selected a moonless night. He was up ahead somewhere on the dirt road. Martin narrowed his eyes and crouched in an effort to locate Egk's outline, but saw only the shapes of crooked telephone poles and humped, grassy banks against the lightening sky. Martin was walking more slowly than he ought, keeping pace with Uwe Wurfel, who trudged near him in distress. 'Are you all right?' he whispered. 'Not fit,' Wurfel gasped. A sheep's cough drove them into a roadside ditch. 'Up you get,' said Martin, and they moved on again. The hours passed and they learned to expect Egk to materialize at a gate or crossroads and hiss directions or complain about lost time.

At dawn he led them off the road and towards a cluster of trees at the top of a rise. They waded through damp spring grasses, wildflowers and tangled flowering weeds that released a poisonous stench under their crushing shoes. Dark water pools lay in the cow pats. 'Keep to the grass,' Egk said. 'Leave no footprints anywhere.' A half-ruined wooden farmhouse stood behind the trees. The wind began to gust with the dawn, and the agitated branches on the imported trees were like tatty witches riding their brooms. There was the smell of approaching rain. 'Mushrooms,' cried Uwe Wurfel. He knelt to pick them but Egk pulled back his arm. 'No evidence,' said Egk. 'Leave no evidence anywhere.' He spoke like this now, every utterance a command or an admonition.

As they neared the rear of the house a flock of pigeons left their nests under the roof and barrelled into the sky. 'Inside,' said Egk. Neglect and dry rot had weakened the house and over the years people had stripped it of serviceable boards and fixtures.

The floors were unsafe. Iron roofing sheets flapped above and small creatures lived in the corners and under the sagging tin ceilings. Egk hurried from room to room and window to window, and finally said, 'We'll watch from here. Don't disturb the dust. Don't disturb anything.' He turned and looked at them. 'We will eat now.'

Egk opened his small case, took out a paper bag, and turned back to peer through the window at the approach roads. Martin and Uwe sat on the floor, resting their backs against the wall. They also had brought with them a small case. 'Only a change of clothes, nourishing food and small personal items,' Egk had said. Each man wore a dark, ill-fitting everyday suit, a hat, and a broad tie knotted under the curling collar of a plain cotton shirt. Martin took out a hard biscuit, some cheese and an apple. He felt tired. There was mud on his shoes. Egk had told him he must simulate any respectable fellow travelling in an era of petrol rationing, but Martin felt exactly like a fugitive. He stretched out his legs and lay on his side among the pigeon droppings to sleep. Uwe Wurfel coughed weakly. 'Sleep now, Uwe,' said Egk. 'Martin, I will wake you four hours from now.'

Egk shook Martin awake at ten o'clock. 'Report anything. *Anything*,' he said.

Martin stared dreamily through the dirty window. A quick rain squall passed across the sky during his watch, flinging drops of rain against the side of the house like handfuls of sand. Heedless sheep moved head-down across the paddocks. When the sun reappeared a noisy community of sparrows came to bicker among the wet trees and shrubs outside the window, their flights and landings shaking down jewels of water. No vehicles or men approached or passed along the roads. The window faced east, and beyond the sparkling, renewed paddocks, roads and fences were ranges of hills. Beyond them, far beyond them and to the north, was Sydney. Egk said he had been given an address in Sydney, of a man who could shelter or advise them or help them get papers. Martin rocked on his heels at the window and thought about that.

He wanted to go home to put things right. They could throw him back into concentration camp again afterwards if they liked. Or prison: his spirit was murderous. Uwe Wurfel should go north and disappear, live in a rain-forest or go west to the opal fields like any old foreigner. Let Egk go with him. Egk was a marked man anywhere else. He dare not reveal his accent: here they think all foreigners are spies. He dare not drive a car, for fear of setting off down the wrong side of the road by mistake one fine morning. Did he think he could simply leave the country? Did he think there were frontiers at all points of the compass with friendly governments on the other side? But Egk had to get to Sydney first, and he needed Martin to drive and do the talking. No trains, Egk had said. The stations would be watched, and they had no tickets, no travel permits, no identity papers. Egk knew of a car, however, stored on blocks in a disused barn; an unsuccessful escapee had reported it to the escape committee. The farmer had also hidden a drum of petrol in the barn. Martin thought that that was probably right: he, too, had hoarded petrol when rationing was introduced. But supposing the car was still there, and they were able to start it, and drive it to Sydney before anyone knew it was missing – what then? I will take the car then, thought Martin. Egk can go underground in Sydney if he likes, find a ship, call himself a Dutchman from Java. Uwe Wurfel can come with me or stay with Egk, that's up to him. Martin laughed aloud. He was like a man planning to give his neighbours a lift to town, not a desperate fugitive.

At two o'clock he woke Uwe Wurfel to take the next four-hour watch. Wurfel was pale and seemed dazed, and in his over-large suit resembled a thin man wearing a fat man's clothes.

'I think I should let you sleep again,' said Martin.

'No, no, I will be all right.'

'If you don't feel well you may wake me.'

'Have your sleep, Martin,' said Wurfel.

At six o'clock they ate again and waited for darkness.

'I think we should fetch the car tonight,' said Martin. 'Uwe is not strong enough for all this walking and sleeping on cold floors.'

'We should let him be the judge of that,' said Egk.

'Yes, don't fuss over me, Martin.'

'I thought,' said Egk, 'that we had agreed.' They would hide in unlikely places near the camp for three days and steal the car on the fourth night; most escapees were caught within three days of escaping, usually at an obvious local railway station, town or farm; if an escapee was still at large after three days the authorities assumed he had left the district and concentrated the search elsewhere: 'Unless you have a better idea,' said Egk.

Martin glowered: this was Egk – not the pariah, not the man with the burdensome secret. 'We could stay here until then,' he said. 'I think we're safe here.'

'One,' said Egk, 'we would get on one another's nerves and grow less vigilant. I see that that is already happening. Two, each move brings us closer to where the car is stored. Three, remaining in one place increases the risk of discovery.'

'So does walking all over the countryside every night and breaking into all these places, I'd have thought.'

Egk smiled. 'We'll separate, shall we? You go your way, I go mine?'

'And me?' said Uwe Wurfel, looking from one man to the other.

'That prospect is not unwelcome,' Martin told Egk. 'I know this country. You would not last five minutes.'

'I know where the car is.'

'I can steal any car, the first car I find.'

'You will blunder like an amateur, make enough noise to wake the dead, steal a car that is in use every day, try to buy petrol without coupons, drive right into the arms of Buffalo Bill.'

'You will crash the car,' said Martin. 'You will drive on the wrong side of the road and get arrested. Your accent will give you away.'

'I could do the talking,' said Wurfel.

'He would get rid of you the first chance he gets. Stick a knife between your ribs or abandon you on the streets of Sydney.'

'Fine,' said Egk. They watched him pick up his case and lean his face to the black window. 'No unwelcome headlights, a clear sky. I will leave now. Shepparton is in that direction. Or, if you prefer it, the camp is in that direction.'

Egk walked to the door. Uwe Wurfel kneeled unhappily in front of his case, packing away his bag of food and fumbling with the clasps. 'I want the car,' Martin called. 'I will take you to Sydney but I want the car after that.'

Egk crossed the room and pointed his finger.

'And until then I am in charge. Is that understood?'

Martin looked away and nodded.

'Then come.'

They descended to the road and walked again through the night, Egk far ahead and Martin in the rear with Uwe Wurfel. Martin concentrated his attention on sounds, for thinking about Egk upset him. Frogs or fishes gulped in the irrigation channels and hunting birds creaked softly by above him. He detected the privation in Uwe Wurfel's breathing and his irregular footsteps. Once a muddled runaway heifer snorted and backed up and bucked its hind legs at them. Martin supposed sourly that Egk had walked past the flighty creature without alarming it. But mostly the night was quiet but for the sounds the walking men made, and Martin lost interest. 'Are you all right?' he whispered. Uwe Wurfel did not reply. They walked on.

They came to a crossroads, where Egk crouched ready for flight, signalling furiously. 'Quiet, for heaven's sake!'

Somewhere a car or truck slowed down and gained speed again.

'Off the road. Quick.'

So much for being respectable working men on their way somewhere. They lay in the mud and water of the roadside ditch while a small car passed by, revealing to the enemy a feeble slit of light from its mantled headlamps.

'Stay down,' Egk hissed.

They waited and eventually Egk said, 'You may come out now.'

'I feel quite cold,' said Uwe Wurfel.

'We must keep going,' said Egk. 'We will change our clothes later.'

They spent the second day in an abandoned pump-house on an irrigation channel. While two men slept the third, dressed now in another suit, would keep watch. The view from the pump-house door was poor, and so Egk advised a cautious circuit of the building from time to time. Nothing disturbed them. To alleviate his boredom Martin scraped the mud from his old suit and shoes and sponged the stains away with canal water. He ate another apple and the remainder of his cheese. What did Egk imagine they would do when the food ran out? Had he a fishing line in his pocket? A catapult with which to knock waterfowl from the sky?

When Egk awoke he stood over Uwe Wurfel, regarding him with displeasure. Wurfel lay exhausted and absolutely still in sleep, but his breathing sounded ragged and fitful.

'He needs a long rest. Or a doctor,' said Martin from the doorway.

'We don't have so far to walk tonight,' said Egk. 'Or tomorrow night. Did you see anything?'

'No.'

Egk smiled and rubbed his palms together. 'It's working.'

'We need food,' said Martin.

'Oh yes,' said Egk. 'Oh yes, I expect so. That does not surprise me in the least.'

'You have been more careful, I suppose. You no doubt calculated to the final mouthful.'

'We will share. Does our friend have any food left?'

'Why don't you wake him and ask?'

'Herr Linke, you are being tiresome.' Egk kneeled and opened Uwe Wurfel's case, took out the bag of food, and combined it with his own. He held up his hand. 'Yours, please.'

'This is all I have.'

'I am not judging you. I am attempting to solve our problem. The door, Martin.'

'There is no one out there. It's almost dark.'

'The door, please, Herr Linke.'

While Egk made up three packets of food, Martin watched the sun-streaked clouds fade to ordinariness on the flat western horizon. Later Egk left the pump-house to fetch drinking water, and as he passed through the door he put something in Martin's hand. 'I don't think we need to divide this,' he said. It was a stale pastry. 'Smile, Martin, for heaven's sake.'

'There is food all around us,' Martin shouted. 'Fish, rabbits, mushrooms, quail, waterhens. Trap me a rabbit if you're so smart.'

They did not leave the pump-house until ten o'clock, allowing Uwe Wurfel to sleep until then. The full moon cast their shadows and Egk, already many yards ahead, was clearly visible. Martin turned to Uwe Wurfel and said, 'I'll carry this for you,' prising the old man's case from his fingers, and when he faced forward again there was no Egk but a gloomy apparition on the road. He knocked Wurfel into the grass.

'Are you mad?'

*'Turn your face away!'*

Then Wurfel heard the irrhythmic rolling of the wheels and the military chassis creaking down upon them, and he lay still. The road barely sloped at all, and the lorry, blunt-faced like an elderly pug, took many seconds to coast past them. They heard the driver apply the brakes and the soldiers jump out and encircle the pump-house. Sometime later, the soldiers shouted and reboarded the lorry, the motor was started with a percussion that beat down upon the men hiding in the grass, and the search-party drove on.

'Where are you?' Egk whispered.

'Here.' Martin helped Uwe to stand.

'Keep low and don't make a sound. They may have left a sentry.' A note of elation was in Egk's voice. He turned and crept away.

'My heart,' said Uwe Wurfel. He smiled at Martin, his hand held flat against his chest. 'At this moment I am confirmed that I have one.'

'My knees have turned to rubber,' said Martin.

They gasped and grinned at each other like clergymen discovering a taste for burglary.

'For once I found myself in a dry ditch,' said Wurfel. 'I suppose we had better move on.'

'How are you feeling now?'

'Years older and years younger, I am not sure which.'

At four o'clock in the morning Egk stopped them and pointed to an indistinct settlement at the roadside ahead of them.

'I have been observing it for some time. It appears to be safe.'

Their third refuge was a small country school inside a tidy white picket fence. One large pine tree sheltered the hard dirt playing area, a rope-and-tyre swing hanging unevenly from a branch, and a line of pine trees separated the school from a community tennis court. A rain-water tank stood behind the lean-to shelter-shed. There was just such a school in the middle of nowhere near Martin's farm. Its image appeared as sharp as the excisions in a stencil plate and he felt intense longing.

Egk examined the ground around the gate in the picket fence and between the gate and the door of the school. 'They searched here also,' he said, 'so you may relax. They will not search here again.'

'But a school,' said Martin.

'It's the weekend,' Egk explained.

'So it is.'

The men slept and kept watch, and in the afternoon four children with raquets and balls appeared on the tennis court behind the school. Between games they wandered into the school yard to drink from the rain-water tank and idle about the building. They rattled the door handle. Their shoes bumped against the outside wall as they endeavoured to pull themselves up to peer through the windows. Their conversations were queer, alien. The escapees remained on the floor under desks until the children drove away in a horse and buggy.

Egk grinned. 'Tonight we take the car.'

'Thank God for that.'

A Sunday night in a rural backwater in wartime: would there be people abroad tonight? Egk wanted to know.

Probably not, they told him.

'Then we shall leave as soon as it is dark.'

They ate sparingly, allowing for their needs on the road to Sydney. Egk had a pocketful of shillings and sixpences, but he said it would be unwise for them to enter a shop before they reached the city. The inconsiderable meal left Martin feeling pinched and dissatisfied.

They left the school at eight o'clock, Egk carrying Wurfel's case for him and walking at a slower pace. By nine o'clock they had reached the barn, an old-fashioned wooden building with double wooden doors and a hayloft. No farmhouse was apparent; grass grew freely on the track leading to the doors.

Once inside the barn, Egk appeared to lose his overmastering air. He did not touch the car – an old black sedan raised upon wooden blocks – but stood back discouraged. 'I am in your hands. I know nothing about these things.'

'I expect the battery has been removed,' said Uwe Wurfel, trembling forth with a candle. Wurfel's vitality was low; his face was composed of eye-sockets and whiskery, depleted skin.

'Does that mean we must now steal a battery? I did not want to attract that kind of attention.'

Egk muttered and paced, keeping close to the wall as though avoiding emanations from the car. His dejection inspired the others and they began an inspection of the car, Martin raising the bonnet and reaching across the engine with a candle, Uwe Wurfel squeezing each of the dusty tyres.

'The tyres are good.'

'Check the spare,' said Martin. 'The radiator has been drained, of course.'

Egk raised his candle. 'The battery?'

'There is one, after all, though disconnected and probably flat. I would not have left the battery in.'

'How will you start it with a flat battery?' said Egk. 'And look at these blocks.' He edged out of the shadows and fretfully kicked one of the four wooden stumps supporting the car. 'They will have to be removed.'

Martin found a wagon jack among the planks, coils of wire, fence posts and tools heaped against the rear wall. With additional support from its own jack, he settled the car by stages onto the barn floor. Uwe Wurfel made repeated trips to a horse trough outside the barn, filling his pannikin with water to pour into the radiator. Egk observed, a pleasureless figure behind a candle.

'It would help,' said Martin, 'if you found some mud and smeared it on the number plates.'

Egk thought, said, 'A good idea, yes,' and followed Wurfel outside.

Martin connected the battery. At first he had been mistrustful of the barn and its contents, expecting traps, bawling voices, flooding lights, the logical end to flight in darkness and criminality, but now he realized that the car's owner had given little thought to thieves and perhaps was even optimistic about using the car again soon. A small drum of petrol was under an empty wheat bag. No attempt had been made to conceal the battery acid and distilled water. Martin reflected warmly upon a fellow much like himself, down to earth, coping with muddles and irritations not of his own making. He would see that the fellow got his car back again.

'What next?'

'Fill the petrol tank and then put the drum in the boot of the car.'

Martin cut and rearranged the wiring so that he could start the car without a key, fitted the crank handle, and turned it. The engine refused to start, and at midnight Egk said, 'I had hoped to drive all night.' Martin felt unthanked and close to anger. 'Your turn,' he said, standing back from the crank-handle. Egk, and then Wurfel, cranked the engine, but without success, and Martin said they would have to push-start the car.

'And if that doesn't work?' said Egk.

'Then we abandon it on the track and the whole world knows we have been here, or we steal a battery.'

Egk laughed and leaned forwards, placing his palms against the car. 'Exactly,' he said, beginning to push.

The engine clashed unnervingly into life a few yards short of the road gate. Martin hurried them away from there, concentrating over the steering wheel at the road, indistinct in the moonlight. Unease clung to them like cobwebs for the remainder of the night and all the next day.

# CHAPTER 17

'I will stop and ask somebody.'

'You said that you knew Sydney,' said Egk from the back seat.

'Everything has changed a little. Nothing is as I remember it.' Martin had driven past the GPO twice before identifying it behind a shell of planks and sandbags. All the familiar structures had been recontoured in this way. Slender gun barrels reached up from swathes of camouflage netting, and everybody wore a uniform of some kind. Soon someone would demand to know how it was that three civilians had the opportunity, time and petrol to be driving around and around the block in this manner.

On the footpath ahead of them several women in headscarves and harassed by small children were standing in line outside a butcher's shop. Martin slowed the car and parked next to a wall poster explaining Britain's need of foodstuffs. He got out of the car.

The woman at the end of the queue wore an overall. That was interesting: possibly she worked in an armaments factory. He said, 'Excuse me, I wonder if you could tell me the way to King's Cross.'

A number of women turned round. All looked at him with tiredness and odium. 'We're lost,' he said. In the old days they would have conferred and taken you by the sleeve and pointed brightly this way and that. Martin glanced uneasily at the car: it had disreputable lines, handprints in the dust and discernible Victorian numberplates.

'What's your game?' one woman said.

'We have business in King's Cross,' said Martin. 'An appointment.'

'Business! That's a good one,' said another woman.

'Nice for some.'

'Life of Reilly.'

'What you got in the car, eh?'

'Madwomen,' said Martin, starting the engine. He steered along streets crowded with people riding bicycles home from work, feeling more vulnerable and out-of-place than at any time since their escape. Then he recognized Hyde Park and drove with relief up to King's Cross. It was early evening.

'Am I to understand,' said Egk, 'that those women thought we were up to no good? I would say this area crawls with criminals and prostitutes.'

'It does have a reputation,' said Uwe Wurfel.

'Look at that.'

A black American soldier had been approached and negotiations were under way.

'Scum.'

'The Negro or the girl?'

But Egk said, 'Park the car where you can, Martin. My contact is not available before eight o'clock, and I think we may treat ourselves to dinner first.'

Martin imagined hot meat and vegetables and cups of strong tea, white table linen and someone waiting upon them. He said with feeling, 'We deserve it.'

'Even I have an appetite,' said Uwe Wurfel, pressing his sparse hair against his skull. Before entering Sydney they had drawn off the road to wash and shave in cold water and look critically at one another's appearance. Egk had opened a small jar. 'A pomade,' he said. 'A pleasant smell to disarm suspicions.' Their heads gleamed.

They ate in the New York Cafe, which had no American customers. The waitress used chewing gum. Martin wanted to express to her his dissatisfaction with the austere menu, but that would only lead to an uncomfortable conversation beginning with, 'Where have you been lately?' He ordered mutton. It came with a trickle of watery gravy, a potato and a sliced carrot, poor, soft, congealing things. Dry bread and a butter substitute were delivered with reluctance when he asked for them. He finished with a small, possibly fake pudding-slice. The waitress was not encouraging about a second cup of tea. Then a party of American sailors asked for a table and she did not come back at all.

'I have eaten better meals you-know-where,' he said.

'Poor, suffering civilians,' said Egk.

Three girls, dressed to appear older, entered the cafe to linger near the Americans' table. 'Hey,' said the Americans, drawing out the word. Egk looked on, amused, as though finding additional confirmation of incaution and decay in the country. He also was able to watch the street door from his chair, and a few minutes later he gripped the edge of the table.

'We will finish now,' he said. 'Pay, and casually leave. No fuss.'

They stood up, Martin positioning his chair neatly under the table to mask his fear. Two men, with the appearance of officials, passing down the cafe; interested, for some reason, in the Americans or their tarts. 'The docket please, miss,' Martin called. Surely they heard, as he did, his lingering accent? He put his hand close to his mouth. 'Righto, love?' he said, or something like it. He put on his hat. Nodded pleasantly and made room in the narrow space. They paid at the cash register while, behind them, voices were being raised.

'Look what the cat's dragged in.'

'Enough of that. Your papers, please.'

'Why don't you crawl back under a stone.'

'Yes, go on. We aren't doing anything. Leave us alone.'

'What's with these guys? Who are these guys?'

'Manpower. Aren't you? Bloody Manpower.'

'I don't get it.'

'You blokes stay out of this. It doesn't concern you. Where do you girls work? Let's see your papers, please.'

'We've got jobs!'

'Go and pick on someone else.'

'I could be wrong, but I'd say you girls have been soliciting.'

There were the sounds of a scuffle and a chair falling. 'Back to the car,' said Egk, 'before that happens to us.'

It had been an article of Martin's faith, during internment, to link the mind to the world outside the wire. He attended

97

lectures, and read travel books, thoughtful books, and the better newspapers and magazines. Avoiding madness, he formed an impression of the world before it went mad. A young man, just down from his university, may walk penniless the length of France, meet dotty aristocrats in mouldy chalets off the beaten track, follow a truffle-digging boar in a forest, speculate about an arrangement of stones on a hillside. East African planters dress for dinner and drink sundowners while drum-beats sound in the evening air. You might meet Somerset Maugham in Tahiti or at Raffles Hotel or on the *Queen Mary*. Men wearing white suits and solar topees ride the river steamers of South America, Levantines run trading posts in jungles, the hill bandits of Afghanistan swoop down on horseback, brandishing flintlock rifles. Not the housekeeper herself, the postman, the baker, the priest, in fact no one in the little Alpine village knew that the shy man living in the cottage on the lake was writing the most important philosophical work of the century. He grew roses, that's all they knew. People and places like these were the geography of Martin's thoughts. On the blinded streets of King's Cross, figures rutted in doorways, lifted their faces to tilted bottles and slid from one hole in the corner to the next. They shrieked and were heartless like his wife.

Egk caught his windmilling arms. 'Stop, Martin. Be calm, be calm.'

'I want,' said Martin, 'to drive you to your spy now, so that I can leave this madhouse.'

'The camp will be our only destination if you panic again.'

Creeping taxis braked on the street and everywhere people entered and re-entered the dingy buildings. On the steps of a hotel a kilted Scottish soldier reached breaking point and directed his fist into a jibing face. Martin, Egk and Wurfel hurried by, unsettled to see so many uniforms massing.

The car was in a dark back street of workers' cottages. As he opened the driver's door, Martin said good evening to a large beery man leaning his forearms on a nearby garden gate, smoking an evening cigarette. The cigarette bobbed in the knocked-about face.

'Bloke was here, what, five minutes ago? Gives your car the once over.'

'I beg your pardon?' said Martin.

'He goes, "This your car?" I go, "What do you reckon." Not five minutes ago.'

'Did he say what he wanted? Did he say where he was going?'

The man removed the cigarette from his mouth and regarded the burning tip.

'I thought, there has to be more to this than meets the eye, so I'll hang around and see what happens. Sure enough, you jokers turn up.'

Egk said stiffly, 'This person. What does he do now?'

The man, alerted, turned to Egk with great interest. 'A bloke could start wondering why you want to know and who you blokes are and whether it mightn't be worth a bob or two, if you get my drift.'

Egk dug in his pocket. 'Here.'

The man looked disparagingly into his palm and said, 'He was a copper, wasn't he. Had to be. Probably on the blower to the CIB by now.'

They took their cases from the car. They heard the man call after them, 'Do you want me to keep an eye on your car?' and a little later, 'Won't breathe a word, all right?'

'Let me think,' said Egk in the next street. 'Martin, you will ask for directions, please. Let us hope it is not a long walk.'

'I will not be coming with you,' said Martin. 'I am shattered by this. I will find the highway, and in the morning stick out my thumb.'

Egk stood chest to chest with him. 'No you won't, Martin. Do you know why? As we stand here talking our friend is making mental notes of our appearance and my accent and calculating their worth in beer money. We will find my contact and listen to what he advises. Now, directions please.' Egk pointed at a boarding house on the corner. 'I suggest you try in there.'

An elderly woman sat inert in an armchair in the small reception lounge. She looked at the case in Martin's hand. 'Full up, love. Sorry. Haven't had a room free for two months.'

Martin explained that he wanted directions and named the street. The woman rocked back and forth in the chair, gaining the momentum to help her stand, and took Martin out to the footpath, where she pointed. 'First right, second left. Not far. Them your friends?' she said. 'Come far?'

'We work for the government.'

The woman at once turned back to the boarding house and closed the door behind her. We are drawing every curious eye, Martin thought, where a man by himself would not be noticed.

'Well?' said Egk.

'It is very near.'

When they reached the street Egk said, 'He is at number nineteen.'

It was a street of deteriorating cottages and small iron foundries, almost lightless since most of the dimmed streetlights were also faulty. Few buildings were numbered. Egk stopped at a collapsed verandah.

'Perhaps you were given the wrong number.'

After a moment Egk said, 'No, this is the place. Martin, will you knock on someone's door and ask, please.'

'We are leaving a trail of witnesses behind us, all over Sydney.'

'What else do you suggest? I have brought us this far,' said Egk tiredly.

'I think you both should wait out of sight,' said Martin.

Next to number nineteen was a narrow shop-front, its lettering faded. Someone lived in the back rooms. Weak light showed behind the tarpaper adhering to a side window. Martin knocked and waited.

'Is that you, Mrs Brooks? Did the siren go?'

Martin put his face close to the door panel. 'Excuse me, I am on leave and thought I would visit my friend Tom Cousins in number nineteen, but I must have the wrong address.'

'Just a minute, just a minute.' An old man dressed for bed opened the door. 'Was that the siren? Where's Mrs Brooks?'

Martin explained again.

'Thought you were the warden,' the old man said. 'No Tom

Cousins around here, not that I know of anyrate. What was the number again?'

'Nineteen.'

'Well there you are then. Are you with the Army?'

Martin said, 'With the government.'

'Ah.' The old man brightened and moved closer like a conspirator. 'I got you. What he said was he worked for one of the radio stations, but we always thought he did something hush hush, didn't we mother?' The old man turned and opened the door a little wider, precipitating sounds of fearful old age in the dark hall behind him.

'Who did?' said Martin.

'Your friend, Tom Cousins,' said the old man.

'I don't think that was his name,' the old woman said.

'I gather he no longer lives there,' said Martin.

'Fellows, friends of his, picked him up a fortnight ago,' said the old man. 'Took his cases with him. You could try his office in the morning.'

'Thank you, I will do that.'

'I don't think they were his friends,' the old woman said.

Martin walked to the end of the street and waited for Egk and Wurfel to join him.

'I would say that he has been arrested.'

'It's the only contact I have,' said Egk.

'What will you do now?'

'What will I do now? Herr Linke,' said Egk, 'what will *we* do now.'

'I am going home,' said Martin.

'Theodor and I were talking just now,' said Uwe Wurfel. 'I suggested we try to reach Cairns. There are places where we can hide, up there. I have friends there.'

'Cairns.'

'Come with us, Martin,' said Egk. 'You will be arrested if you go home. They will be waiting for you.'

'Uwe can do the talking for you now. I have done enough.'

'I think you should know,' said Egk confidingly, leading

101

Martin away by the elbow, 'Herr Wurfel is very ill. I believe he may be dying.'

'He's not dying.' Martin peered round at Wurfel.

'Help me take him home, Martin.'

'Don't you realize how far it is to Cairns? You will never make it.'

'They will be waiting for you, Martin. Come with us. Hide with us until it is safe for you to return.'

A whispering voice, saturated with falsity. Even Uwe Wurfel, a lame, uncertain shape in the gloom, seemed tainted. When Wurfel coughed then, Martin hated the sound of it; but he said, to expiate his pettiness:

'If you like I will accompany you both as far as Casino. Then you are on your own.'

'I suggest we try a train,' said Egk.

# CHAPTER 18

It was possible that the guards watched for suspicious types dodging behind rolling stock with cameras or pencil stubs and paper scraps, or people attempting to ride the passenger trains without a pass, but not those who might sneak aboard a wagon loaded with bully beef cans. Martin listened as a guard tramped by outside. Uwe Wurfel shivered, cold and afraid in their wood-and-iron vault. Egk draped his coat over Wurfel's shoulders. It was very late. Sometime tonight this train would leave for Brisbane. Martin had no reason to doubt the railway official who had told him this. He was the kind of fellow who peers past your shoulder for spies while revealing every vital secret, as though he believed you yourself could not be a spy if you were talking to him.

The train heaved massively, every coupling taking up the strain, and by degrees moved out of the station. Cans of bully beef clacked in their crates.

'I must make water,' said Uwe Wurfel. 'I am sorry, I must. The coldness has reached into my bones.'

He edged, in an attitude of shame and panic, into a gap between the crates and the far end of the wagon.

'You must not apologize, Uwe,' said Egk. 'I understand.' As though Martin did not.

Martin ignored them; sat, feeling unreproved, unreproached, on a cushion of his folded clothes on the wagon floor. He closed his eyes. This was the final stage. He had a sense of something nearly at an end. He pictured the continent, their train a black speck creeping up the eastern coast. Not so very far to go, hardly any distance at all, but a movement northwards on a map seemed to Martin a movement uphill, and so the train laboured.

The train stopped often, delivering and collecting boxes,

packages and mailbags. Martin got up to investigate. The stations were unnamed – to foil, he supposed, the Japanese invader. For the moment that was not a problem; he would sleep now, and later, when it was daylight, begin studying every station, bridge and hill until he identified the approach to Casino. When the train slowed, he would jump out.

He sat down again. Here in the rattling wagon he was undisturbed by human turbulance. After days of movement and disarray, he began to feel composed. He was also pleased with himself. In a state of chaos and perturbation he had let himself be led through the wire and follow Egk and do Egk's bidding, Egk insistent and certain of his power, but since then there had been too many emergencies where only Martin had saved them. He smiled. Telling people he was with the government had been an inspired idea.

The train pulled through the night. Egk and Wurfel were silent, either asleep or battered into quiescence by the noise, draughts and unyielding floor. He would be free of them soon. He pictured what they would see: the sliding doors rolled back on their castors; the wagon floor, walls and roof framing the dawn light; Martin flickering into the open space; Martin tensing to leap. They would close the doors behind him and retire once more to the shadows, taking up positions to help them endure the journey and their intimations of approaching catastrophe.

For they would not make it beyond the coal-packed rails and sleepers of the Brisbane shunting yards. Martin knew that he himself would soon be in custody. But, first, he would observe and assess the running of his farm, and, at the end of the day, when eveyone was at home, make his way into the town and confront the so-called guardians of his children and deal with their so-called mother.

It was morning. Martin exercised his arms, legs and neck, and opened one of the doors to peer out.

'Are we almost at your town?' said Egk.

Martin said, 'I expect so. I will soon know for certain.'

The train slowed and cautiously crossed a viaduct spanning

a gorge of bulrushes. Martin closed the door and returned to his seat on the floor. 'About one hour from now.'

Egk left his corner and began to rearrange some bully beef crates near Martin into the form of a long bench seat. Now we look like fugitives, Martin thought, looking at Egk. Red raddle from the hieroglyphics identifying the crates had smeared Egk's trousers and sleeves. The knot in his tie looked tight, immovable, from too many adjustments. He had lost his hat. At some point in the past five nights the sole of one shoe had come loose and Egk frequently had to prise out pebbles and twigs. Martin looked at his own shoes and clothes. He had been reduced just as much.

Egk helped Uwe Wurfel to get up from the floor, and they sat next to Martin on the crates. Fourteen months earlier – also on a train, and at about this same spot – Wurfel had turned to Martin a spirited, canny face and advised disbelief. Now he was attached to his persecutor, to whom he kept affirming, 'In Cairns . . .,' and trepidation creased his face. He could well die. Martin thought it deliberately.

'About one hour, you say,' said Egk, crossing his legs like a man on a park bench.

'Yes.'

'And Uwe and I will bid you farewell and continue on to Brisbane.'

'The official told me Brisbane, yes.'

'Where we jump out and locate a train going to Cairns – avoiding the guards, of course.'

'Yes.'

Egk leaned forward. 'But our chances are poor, don't you think? We had some control when we had the car; now we are at the mercy of any halfwit blundering around a corner to smoke a cigarette.'

'I am getting off,' said Martin.

'I know that,' said Egk. 'And you intend to walk with your eyes open into the arms of the authorities. Fine. I will not dwell on it. But I do not wish to be caught.'

'Nor do I,' said Uwe Wurfel.

'Nor does Uwe.'

'I would not survive,' Wurfel said.

'You might be lucky,' said Martin. 'You might not be challenged. If you are, let Uwe do the talking. You could pass as cracked old swagmen too difficult to be bothered with.'

'Or we could drive,' said Egk.

'Steal a car? If you want to take the risk. Look, I am sorry, it is all up to you now.'

Egk picked at the wood splinters in his fingers. 'Do you own a car or truck, Martin?'

'I beg your pardon?'

'On your farm. Is there a farm vehicle perhaps, something that you have stored in a shed?'

'There is,' said Uwe Wurfel. 'He once told me about it.'

'My God. Do not think you are getting off with me. I am not driving you anywhere.'

'Think, Martin. Do you really want to go back to the camp? You might even be arrested before you are able to see your children. Come with us, return when the risk is less.'

'I am not listening to you. I don't wish to talk about it.'

Egk put his hand gently on Martin's shoulder and said, 'Then will you let me take the car, please, Martin? Look at Herr Wurfel. He should not have to endure any more of this.'

Martin pulled away, stood up, rolled open one of the doors. He watched the unvarying paddocks and country roads and scrub until he recognized a level-crossing where, years ago, while driving home a new second-hand tractor, he had encountered a train and panicked with the unfamiliar controls.

Five minutes. He gauged the distance between his case and the door, and the time it would take him to repack the case, rush with it to the door, slide open the door, judge a landing place, leap. But Egk was watching him. Before he had even begun, Martin felt himself burdened by the kind of elaborate casualness that deceives no one. He returned to his seat, leaving the door ajar.

'Soon?'

'Half an hour or so.'

'Half an hour.'

Egk opened and closed the lid of his case and settled it by his feet. Then he began attending to Uwe Wurfel, speaking to him in a low voice, encouraging him with smiles and a slap on the knee. And so they were ready when Martin leapt, caseless, through the open door.

# CHAPTER 19

They lay under a pine tree whose lower branches had been scorched by fire. Every summer the railway gangers walked along the line with matches and knapsacks, burning off the dry grass, and every summer the flames got away from them. In remembering this, and seeing the distant station-master's house and water-tower from an unexpected angle, Martin sensed, briefly but intensely, that the town was absurd and his seventeen years in it a farce. He breathed in the smell of pine needles and dewy grass. Egk was speaking, explaining still how they would help one another, as though there had been no interlude. Uwe Wurfel was touching the tip of one finger to his swelling ankle. He could not walk on it.

'Then tonight,' Egk said, 'after you help me start the car I will drive it here, collect Uwe, and we will be on our way.'

'I am sorry to be such a nuisance, Theodor.'

'We will take good care of the car. Somehow we will get it back to you.'

Martin turned his attention to them. He understood that Egk intended to escort him to the farm and wait with him among the trees that overlooked it. With an effort he said: 'If, as you say, they are watching my place, don't you think you should hide here with Uwe? I could bring the car to you.'

Egk smiled. 'Now Martin,' he said, 'I think two pairs of hands and eyes will be better than one.'

Uwe Wurfel said, 'I will be all right during the day. Sleep and rest will do me good.'

At least that would be one of them out of the way. Martin crouched and listened. 'Time to go. Before too many people are about.'

Wurfel was filled with emotion. He said, 'Goodbye, old

108

friend. May we meet again in happier circumstances,' and allowed his right hand to tremble up. Martin touched his to it briefly.

'I will return when it is dark,' said Egk. 'Here is some food. Now, stay hidden, and rest your foot.'

'Time is wasting,' Martin said.

Egk followed Martin across the tracks, through a fence, and down to the river's edge, hard at his heels and alert for another ruse. They plunged onto a path; willow and river gum roots lay exposed along it like clenched arms. Reeds choked the river side of the path, opposite trees tangled with vines and creepers. As Martin and Egk parted the fronds and tendrils, thistledown floated free behind them. Martin could smell the onionweed. This part of the river ran like a rim round half of the town, meeting it at the orderly park and children's playground behind them, then curving through these weeds and trees, and finally branching away at the cemetery near his farm. He could think of no better way to skirt the town and reach his house without attracting suspicion. He looked up at the ridge, at the backyard fences eaten up with rust, the runnels of sewage in the onionweed; this was where your rag-and-bone men, seasonal shearers and poor widows lived. They kept hens and engineless car bodies behind the house and would not look twice at two down-at-heel fellows following the river. Your Frank Lucases would bring in the children and telephone the police.

At the cemetery bend he pointed wordlessly up at the pine trees that sheltered the graves, and led Egk towards them, away from the river. They climbed through a fence that was in better condition that most of the graves. The little rails were rusty, the dead flowers like weeds in the jam jars. Weeds collared the tilting headstones. Here and there gold leaf lettering gleamed on the soupy marble. The dirt was red and already summer-dry, speckled with minute worn stones and black and brown ants. But the familiar names on the stones in the main rows went back generations, and Martin wanted to push them over with his foot. They crossed to the other side, to an area some distance from the graves and obscured by boxthorn bushes.

'This is where we wait.'

Egk looked down at a road and the collection of buildings beyond it. 'That is where you live? Your farm?'

'Yes.'

'Where is the car stored?'

Martin gestured at one of the sheds. 'Over there.' He did not want to go into it again. He was intent on pin-pointing irregularities and meddling. The flower beds were in good order; the hedge needed a trim; a child's tricycle – it was not Paul's, but Martin was reminded of his son's thin pedalling legs – had carelessly been left outside all night. The yard and sheds looked to be tidy. The sun flashed so strongly on the greenhouses that he thought it possible one of the Italians had washed down the glass. The orchard, the farm's farthest point, was unchanged, but, closer to, in the small vegetable fields, the authorities had had their victory over his basil, garlic, zucchini and artichokes. There had not been many people who understood about artichokes.

Between eight o'clock and half past eight three cars stopped at the house. The first pulled into the driveway and sounded its horn. A minute later a woman and three children left the house, the two boys with black wet hair combed for school, and were driven away. 'They were natives,' said Egk. 'Did you know that you had natives living in your house?' The second car parked on the edge of the road a short distance from the front gate. The driver got out and leaned one foot on the bumper bar to smoke a cigarette. Sergeant Richards and a constable were in the third car. They stopped to talk to the man smoking the cigarette, drove in and made a circuit of the yard and sheds, and returned to the town. At midday and again at four o'clock a different man took over the watch. Sergeant Richards returned once. Also at four o'clock a car came by and dropped the woman and her children at the front gate. The little girl put her hands on her hips and said something to her brothers. They entered the house. 'I wonder what it's like inside,' said Egk. A few minutes later, the children, dressed in old clothes, left the house and began to play, and then the woman came out with a cup and saucer, which she took to the man on duty. He put down his newspaper. Martin wondered if the same pattern was being followed at Jean's house and the house where Betty now lived.

'We will see what happens at eight o'clock,' said Egk. 'There might not be a night watch.'

'But the people in the house will hear the car. So will the Italians.' Martin pointed. 'They are quartered in that shed. I wish that you would just go away.'

'I don't think the Italians are there any more. There has been no sign of them. Why are they not in the fields? I see,' Egk added, 'that you have a telephone.'

'Yes, which is why you should give up this idea.'

'I will cut the line. Where are you going?'

'To find a tap to drink from. There is no need for you to follow me.'

'Oh, but I am thirsty,' said Egk.

Martin put his arm inexpertly around Egk's neck. They began to turn round and round in the dirt, their shoes scrabbling. They fought like this until Egk stumbled and overbalanced, pitching them both onto their knees on the ground. Neither man had the energy to resume fighting. They rested, and later sought a tap for water, without speaking to one another. We are like marriage partners, Martin thought. If we had been strangers Egk would have said – just now, and on the train this morning – 'Who do you think you are? How dare you?' and I would act with more confidence, but we know one another too well. And so I must wait and help him with the car or never be rid of him. He folded his coat into a pillow and attempted to sleep. He felt restless, distracted by hunger.

'Martin, he is driving away.'

Egk was staring at the house. It was quite possible that he had sat motionless for three hours, while the sun set and the moon came out. 'Is it eight o'clock?' Martin said.

'No one has come to take over from him.'

Martin stood up, but Egk reached out and clasped his wrist. 'Not yet. We should wait a little longer.'

111

'My God,' said Martin. He wanted to perform a small, tight dance of hunger.

'Sit down, Martin. Come, sit here. It will soon be over.'

Martin sat and rocked, his cheek against his knees.

'You will soon see your children. Will you have far to walk?'

'No, for God's sake.'

'I should not want Uwe Wurfel to be exposed for too long, you see.'

'I am not driving you there. Understand that. Unless you steer into the river you can be with him in just five minutes.'

Well, no, Egk did not mean that. He explained, as they walked by moonlight down to the house, that it would be best if he made his own way now. He had most of the information he needed. Would Martin please tell the authorities where to find Herr Wurfel?

# CHAPTER 20

'Hartley.'

'Jesus. I'll go and fetch Jean.'

Hartley tugged up his braces and edged around the stove and kitchen dresser and through the door without presenting his back to Martin. He had been rinsing cups and saucers under the tap.

'I am not dangerous,' Martin said.

The ten o'clock news was on the wireless, war news, but Martin had no interest in it. He remembered the smell of the kitchen, and ritualistically looked at the scalloped pink light shade on the pressed-tin ceiling, as though he were paying an idle visit in the days before people had been turned by the war complex.

Jean hurried into the kitchen and kissed his cheek. She held tight to his arms and looked into his face, stepping back when she saw his discoloured teeth and caught the odour of his sooty suit.

'What have you done, Martin? You're taking an awful risk coming here. They said you might. They told us days ago that you might come here, and then when you didn't come we thought you might have gone into hiding or something.'

'It was very difficult.'

'But what will you do? You can't stay here. They check with us every day and I can't hide you.'

Hartley said, 'They telephone every night about this time as well.'

Martin stepped away from Jean and pointed. 'When they telephone tonight don't say anything. They can do what they like with me tomorrow morning, but I need a few more hours first.'

Hartley gestured. 'Whatever you say. You're the boss.'

'Hours for what, Martin? What are you going to do?'

'I want her address.'

113

'Address?' said Hartley.

Jean regarded Martin. 'I don't have her address,' she said. 'You just leave things be.'

'Am I to knock on every door of the town to find her? Don't lie.' Martin pushed at her. 'A stupid lie,' he said, pushing again, advancing as she stumbled backwards. 'Stupid. Stupid.'

'Stop it. Just stop it and listen a moment.'

'Here, steady on, Martin,' Hartley said.

'Betty's in Brisbane. She went to get a job on the American base.'

'You let her take the children to Brisbane?'

'Shh,' said Jean. Hartley listened at the door.

'I will never see them again.'

'She bloody hasn't got the children,' said Hartley. 'They're still here with us.'

Jean said helplessly, 'You know what she's like.'

'She doesn't want kids along, cramping her style.'

'I am sorry,' said Martin, 'I am sorry that I frightened you.' He sat down at the table. He did not know what his feelings were, or to what or whom they had a bearing.

Hartley turned off the wireless. The old clock next to the flour canister ticked frantically. Jean said, 'You must be starving. Are you?'

'I had a letter from you that tipped the balance. Otherwise I would still be in the camp.'

'Well, she changed her mind.'

The telephone began to ring in another room. Jean moved to the door. 'I don't know what to do. If we let you stay tonight will you give yourself up in the morning?'

'I have come here for nothing.'

'I won't say anything, but you'd better not let us down. Martin's hungry, Hartley,' she said.

She left the room. Hartley moved about the kitchen. He put bread, butter, chutney and cold mutton on the table, and water into the kettle. 'If it was up to me I'd tell them,' he said. 'You can't just come in here like this, upsetting everybody. I don't want my kids to see you in the morning, understand?' He sat down and looked with interest at Martin. 'I wouldn't mind betting there's a good reason why you lost those appeals. The old heart still stirs, eh Martin? Well you've gone and buggered up your chances this time. I'd say you're in for the duration.'

'Where are the Italians?' said Martin. 'I didn't see the Italians today.'

'You were at the farm?'

'All day I watched it.'

'The manager took them away somewhere. They couldn't leave them there with you still out.'

Martin savoured his mutton and chutney sandwich. His children were safe. He saw that his brother-in-law was comical. He said, 'So many unsuspected qualities. Now I am a leader of spies and revolts.'

Hartley watched him, sour and distrusting. Finally he said, 'A little gratitude wouldn't go amiss.'

'Therefore I will make the tea,' said Martin, getting up to fetch the boiling kettle.

'We've spent hours on your affairs.'

'I am very grateful.'

'Your house would be a wreck by now if we hadn't put people in it.'

'Only a poor black woman would live in a spy's house,' said Martin.

'It's spotless inside,' Hartley said. 'She's a very fine woman.'

Martin was grave and courteous. He poured tea into three cups, offered one to Hartley, and returned to his meal.

Jean re-entered the kitchen. 'Oh good,' she said, 'you've got something to eat.' She sat down with them. 'Sergeant Richards will drop by about lunchtime as usual. We'll tell him you only just arrived.' She shook her head. 'All that way because you were worried about the children. I'd tell the police that if I were you,' she said. 'It proves you're not dangerous or anything.'

'What about the other two blokes? Where are they?'

'We parted,' said Martin.

He had forgotten about Wurfel. Wurfel could wait.

'You must be exhausted,' said Jean. 'There's a bed in the sleepout you can use. Hartley,' she said, speaking as though Martin should not hear her, 'run the bath for Martin.'

Martin laughed. 'I would frighten the children out of their wits looking like this.'

Hartley left the room. After a while Jean said, 'It hasn't been easy for them. The children at school are terribly cruel sometimes. Even my own children, I'm ashamed to say. It got so bad I moved them into the spare room together.'

'Both of you have been very good to us.'

'So I don't know how to put this. We didn't tell them about your escape – we thought it would only confuse them.'

'Yes.'

'So can you see how upsetting it will be if they find you here in the morning?'

'Upsetting to see their own father?'

'In the circumstances, yes. I think it would be best if you stay out of the way until they're at school. They need never know.'

'You want them to forget me.'

'Don't be silly. I don't want them upset.'

'Before I know it you will send them to Brisbane. You think an immoral waster is better for them than a Nazi.'

'Oh grow up, for goodness sake.'

Paul opened the door and said, 'I can't sleep.' His pyjamas were twisted this way and that. He stared at Martin.

Nina appeared behind him, saying, 'You come back to bed. Sorry, Auntie Jean.'

She glanced at the visitor as though to express an apology, and saw who he was. Her face grew closed and absorbed. She had unbraided her hair. Threaded in the gathered wrists and collar of her nightdress were pale yellow ribbons.

'It's Dad,' Paul said, pointing suddenly. He looked back at Nina. 'That's Dad.'

Jean clapped her hands. 'Off to bed now, both of you. It's late.'

116

'What's Dad here for?'

'Is he home now?'

'We'll talk about it in the morning,' said Jean, turning them around.

'Why is he here?'

'He's been allowed home for a short visit. You can see him in the morning. It's late.'

It was out of Martin's hands. Their voices receded to another part of the house, and he was left with a likeness of them, an outline struck against the light that pours through an open door.

And so he followed them. At the door to their bedroom he said to Jean, 'I will kiss them goodnight.'

'*Martin*!'

'Just a kiss goodnight.'

The children's beds were separated by a brown carpet off-cut. The wardrobe was massive, its mirror spotty and silvered. In a club chair at the foot of Nina's bed sat a doll with a white, unlovely face. Paul owned a chart of military aircraft silhouettes. Not even an internee with barbed wire disease was so impoverished.

The children lay still and quiet as Martin leaned down to kiss them.

'Your old father is a bit dirty, isn't he? I've come a very long way.'

Paul said, 'When are you going back to the gaol?'

'Sometime tomorrow.'

The children eased deeper into their beds.

'But it's not a gaol. You must not listen to people who say your father is in a gaol.'

He hemmed and hawed on the carpet strip between their beds.

'Did you get the pictures I sent you?' He looked around at the room. 'You should have them on the walls. Didn't you like them?'

Nina made adjustments to her top sheet. Paul sat up and pointed at the wardrobe. 'We've got some in there,' he said.

Martin told them it was late; it was time they were asleep. He said goodnight and switched off the light. Disburdened, they brightly cried, 'Goodnight.'

# CHAPTER 21

When they were all asleep he left the house. He smelt of harsh soap and hair oil. His face was smooth. He carried a string bag of bread, apples, and cold roast mutton and potatoes. He wore Hartley's clothes, the mismatching trousers, coat and shirt that Jean had laid out for him to wear in the morning. He crossed the town. The night was reduced to the moon and a dog barking, and to a dry fallen leaf that pursued him in a wind gust, frightening him.

There was no watch on the farm; his house was silent and dark. He walked across the yard to the implement shed, a long open structure in which he kept a small crawler tractor, a plough, kerosene and petrol drums, plough shares and tools. They were in good condition. Next to the far wall was the Dodge, resting upon stacked bricks. This wall was a common wall with a small, windowless stone building in which he stored bags of seed and fertilizer. It had a heavy wooden door. The door was closed, bolted from the outside.

Martin stood listening outside the door. He extended his foot, scraped his shoe along the ground, and at once the sounds of effort behind the door subsided. A length of wire, hooked but worthless, was snatched back through a hole above the latch.

Martin returned to the implement shed and fitted a jack to the rear of the Dodge. He raised it, removed the bricks from under each back wheel, and stacked them against the wall. Egk would be running through the possibilities.

Martin could not wait. He walked back to the seed shed door.

'I will leave them a note,' he said. 'I would not want you to be lost and forgotten, a skeleton for those children to find.'

This time Egk said nothing, and that was Martin's only disappointment.

He returned to the car and removed the blocks from under the front wheels. He was thankful that he had moonlight for he had forgotten to look for a candle or lantern when he left Jean's house. He pumped petrol into the petrol tank, and filled four jerry cans with petrol. He loaded the jerry cans into the boot of the car, next to a shovel, a length of rope and a bagful of tools. In the generator shed there was a bank of fully-charged batteries. He selected one and fitted it to the car. The spare key was in an empty tobacco tin under the front seat. Martin turned on the ignition, adjusted the choke and pushed the starter button, repeating this operation until the engine caught and ran smoothly five minutes later. The noise was enough to wake the widow and her children and the dead in the cemetery.

Martin drove around the town's edge until he came to the station shunting yard. He parked the car and walked towards the trees. He was led to Uwe Wurfel's hiding place by the sound of the fellow's breathing, a sound of strain and fear. He said, 'Uwe,' and Wurfel emerged, limping, carrying a branch.

'I expected to find you asleep.'

'Asleep! The trains have not stopped. Guns and men, hour after hour. Why are you here, Martin? Is Theodor with you?'

Martin explained about Egk. He helped Wurfel to climb through the fence, and gave him support for the walk to the car.

'This is unnecessary trouble for you,' said Wurfel. 'Why didn't you do what Egk suggested?'

'We are going to Cairns.'

'Oh.'

'But a small detour first.'

Instead of turning right after the level crossing Martin turned left, into the deserted main street, and parked outside Lucas's Emporium.

'If anyone comes,' he said, 'sound the horn once.'

Martin broke into the shop through a side window in the alley. He robbed Frank Lucas of clothing, blankets, candles, a small paraffin stove, enamel mugs, a billy and cutlery. He selected a pair of boots. To add insult, he filled a pillowcase with useless gewgaws.

He returned to the car, started the engine, and at once began to yawn.

'I had better talk to you,' Wurfel said, 'to keep you awake.'

Martin turned the car around and drove through the town, approaching its farthest edge, where the back roads had their origin.

'Egk actually said that, that he was going to Cairns alone?'

'Yes.'

'I'm surprised to see you,' said Wurfel. 'Were your children not there?'

'They were there.'

'With their mother?'

'No.'

'Are they in good hands?'

'Yes.'

'Even so,' Wurfel said, 'I had not thought that you would take this risk.'

Martin did not explain that he continued to yield to a private lunacy because of his children. They lived in a dull room in a hot country, and hid the evidence of their odd father under the shoes they removed at the end of the day. They had want of someone who could stand against brutes and run through fire and water.

ALSO BY GARRY DISHER

# PERSONAL BEST

*Thirty Australian authors choose their best short stories*

## EDITED BY GARRY DISHER

In most short story anthologies, an editor decides upon an author's best or most representative story. But what do the writers themselves think?

*Personal Best* breaks new ground in inviting thirty Australian writers to select and explain their best or favourite story. Here are early stories, new stories, famous stories—and a host of unexpected choices. Furthermore, in discussing the stories' origins and how they were made, the contributors to *Personal Best* give a fascinating glimpse of the writer at work.

This anthology represents the best: our best authors choosing their best stories. Contributors include: David Malouf, Elizabeth Jolley, Frank Moorhouse, Kate Grenville, Peter Carey, Barbara Hanrahan, Gerald Murnane, Beverley Farmer, Robert Drewe, Glenda Adams, Helen Garner...and many others.

Absorbing and entertaining, *Personal Best* is the ideal introduction to contemporary Australian short story writing.

# PERSONAL BEST 2

*Stories and Statements by Australian Writers*

### EDITED BY GARRY DISHER

Why do writers write? How do they craft their stories? What do they value in their own work?

When the first *Personal Best* volume appeared in 1989, it broke new ground—here were thirty outstanding short stories chosen and introduced by the writers themselves.

The response was immediate and enthusiastic. The *Sunday Herald* called it 'a brilliant collection'. The *Australian Book Review* said the authors' notes were 'full of intimate detail, hard thinking, quirky humour and incisive criticism'.

*Personal Best 2* offers the same rewards: brilliant stories and absorbing insights into the writing process.

Stories by: Janette Turner Hospital, Rosemary Creswell, Rod Jones, Geoffrey Dean, Gwen Kelly, Brian Dibble, Jane Hyde, Antigone Kefala, Damien Broderick, Kerryn Goldsworthy, Inez Baranay, Kris Hemensley, Barry Dickins, Marion Campbell, Vasso Kalamaras, Brian Matthews, Peter Cowan, Marion Halligan, Judy Duffy, Ania Walwicz, Laurie Clancy, John Hanrahan, Michèle Nayman, Thomas Shapcott, Nicholas Jose, John Morrison, Marian Eldridge, Amy Witting, Bruce Pascoe and Peter Corris.